HOPE
in our villages, towns & cities

DO MORE.
DO IT TOGETHER.
DO IT IN WORD AND ACTION.

HOW TO USE THIS RESOURCE PUBLICATION

This publication is not designed to be read front to back but covers a wide range of information that you can dip in and out of, reading the chapters as they interest and concern you.

Each chapter that relates to a HOPE 08 'high point' has an introduction explaining what it is about and is followed by a Great Ideas section. HOPE 08 is not prescriptive but we wanted to provide you with some ideas to get you thinking and to spark your own creative process – feel free to take the ideas and run with them or to do something completely different!

We've also pulled together as many resources as possible that will help you understand what word and deed mission is about and enable you to make it happen. The Resources section at the back is split into the headings of the chapters so you can easily find the books, training courses, websites and publications that relate to each topic. These will help you put the ideas into practice or give you some more food for thought.

The HOPE 08 website is constantly being updated with fresh ideas, new resources and more information. While we've tried to include as much as we can in this publication the website is able to be more dynamic and gives an opportunity for you to have your say too. We'd love it if you added your own ideas, things that have worked well for your church and community and any lessons you have learned along the way. Just visit www.hope08.com and tell us what you've been up to!

INSIDE HOPE

in our villages, towns & cities

SECTION TWO

Big ideas 20

High Points:

SECTION THREE

If we, God's people, are united in offering ourselves to God to reach and touch those around us, we have the potential to see him change the history of the United Kingdom.

Planning and Preparing   104

SECTION FOUR

Resources & Acknowledgements   134

Editor/writer: Liza Hoeksma
Managing Editors: Steve Clifford and Laurence Singlehurst

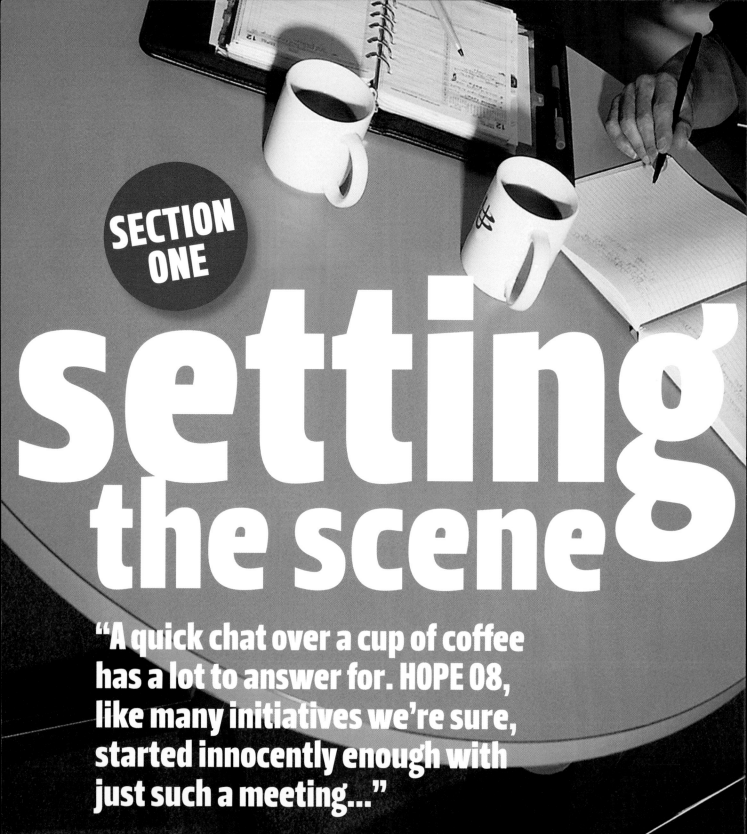

setting the scene

"A quick chat over a cup of coffee has a lot to answer for. HOPE 08, like many initiatives we're sure, started innocently enough with just such a meeting..."

CHAPTER 1

THE STORY SO FAR

**Roy Crowne (Youth for Christ),
Andy Hawthorne (The Message),
Mike Pilavachi (Soul Survivor)**

How did we get into HOPE 08?

A quick chat over a cup of coffee has a lot to answer for. HOPE 08, like many initiatives we're sure, started innocently enough with just such a meeting. We'd been learning about evangelism, outreach and community engagement over a number of years through events large and small like The Message 2000 in Manchester and had just finished our latest harebrained scheme of getting over twenty thousand young people to descend on London for SOULINTHECITY. We were amazed at all God had done in those ten days but the question we couldn't get away from was 'where next?' And that's when we got the bug. Why do *one* thing, for *one* week in *one* city when the *whole* church could rise to the challenge of reaching the *whole* nation for a *whole* year and beyond?

We started talking to others, sharing our passion and vision to see the country changed and were amazed at the response. Rather than telling us we were crazy and it was never going to happen, people of every denomination, stream and ministry started saying 'count us in'. Much as we'd love to take the credit for it, we know the reason everyone has been behind this idea is because it's the great commission that Jesus left us; it's all about reaching the nation with his love.

Why do one thing, for one week in one city when the whole church could rise to the challenge of reaching the whole nation for a whole year and beyond?

The HOPE 08 vision

The dream is to change a nation. Admittedly it's not a small dream but since when did God ever tell us to aim small? We worship a wonderful God who we know loves every single one of the sixty million plus people living in England, Ireland, Scotland and Wales. He longs to reach out to each one of them and has poured out enough resources into his church to do just that. We've got all we need at our disposal but we don't have all the time in the world; we have only our short lifetimes with which to make a difference.

The church has been hidden for too long. We're known by many for pointing the finger on moral issues and collecting money for church renovations. We're seen as a dying, old-fashioned institution so why don't we blow our cover in style? What would happen if in 2008 every community saw the life of Jesus displayed through the passion and actions of thousands upon thousands of Christians? Wouldn't it be amazing if everywhere people looked there were Christians getting involved with their community, finding out its needs and being ready to take action? What would happen if people were to see the church as the Bible teaches it is meant to be; reflecting the love and passion of God? If we, God's people, are united in offering ourselves to God to reach and touch those around us, we have the potential to see him change the history of the United Kingdom.

The values

• To do more in 2008. More than we've ever done before.

• To follow Jesus' example and preach the good news in both word and deed.

• It's not about 'hit and run' evangelism or one-off service projects but about getting involved in our communities to bring lasting change.

• HOPE 08 isn't an event that is being put on, it's a catalyst to help and support each of us as we respond to the needs around us.

• It is flexible so that you can join with churches in your village, town or city to find out what your area needs and respond accordingly.

• Everything we do should be steeped in prayer as we seek God's power and presence as we go.

The headlines

HOPE 08 isn't about us telling you what to do – as we're the first to admit, we don't have all the answers. What we do want to do is provide a network to support you and resources such as this publication that will give you ideas and help you to put them into practice. The year of HOPE will have five high points of focused activity to keep the momentum of mission up and make the most of the opportunities annually given to us. These are:

• **January: Fresh HOPE** – exploring opportunities for people to make a fresh start and attend courses relating to their marriage, parenting, finances, health and fitness. (See Chapter 4.)

• **March/Easter: The Big HOPE** – this will focus on making the celebration of Easter accessible to all in the community. (See Chapter 5.)

• **May: HOPE on the Streets** – throughout the year we're challenging Christians to join together to give one million hours of kindness to our communities. Around the time of Pentecost and over the May

Get involved in any way you can – don't let anything stop you from following God's call to reach out to those around you and show them his love, demonstrating it in all you say and do. Don't keep it to yourself, get others involved; share ideas, pool resources and do everything in his name.

Bank Holiday weekend we'll be focusing on this and finding many practical ways to serve our communities. (See Chapter 6.)

• **September: HOPE Explored** – this is a great chance to invite the whole community to discuss the Christian faith through a whole range of exploratory courses such as Alpha, Christianity Explored, Emmaus, The Y Course and others. (See Chapter 7.)

• **December: The Gift of HOPE.** Christmas is a great time to get creative and explore the opportunities that the celebration of Jesus' birth brings. (See Chapter 8.)

These are the high points of the year but there is loads more you can do and we hope this publication gives you all the ideas you need to get started. We're so glad to have you on board with the HOPE 08 vision and working as part of the team. Get involved in any way you can – don't let anything stop you from following God's call to reach out to those around you and show them his love, demonstrating it in all you say and do. Don't keep it to yourself, get others involved; share ideas, pool resources and do everything in his name. This isn't about putting on the most spectacular events or building the name of HOPE 08; let's devote the year and our lives to spending ourselves in building the kingdom of God and glorifying Jesus.

God Bless

Roy, Andy and Mike

PS: Even as we prepare for 2008, let's prayerfully look even further ahead. Everything we learn and develop that works well for our churches and communities should become a part of the life and rhythm of our church in the years to come.

HOPE 08 is designed to be inclusive of all age groups but there will be special resources including the website:
www.hope-revolution.com
and the myspace site:
www.myspace.com/thehoperevolution
to support and enable young people to get involved with HOPE 08.
See Chapter 9 for more information on The HOPE Revolution – Seeding a youth movement

You don't have to wait until 2008!

Get involved as soon as possible to make HOPE 08 all that it can be in your village, town or city.

Sign up as a partner church – let us know you're on board by registering at www.hope08.com. We'll keep you up to date through our regular e-newsletters featuring stories, fresh resources and points for prayer.

Find out about your community – as early as you can, find out as much as you can about your community to make sure your HOPE 08 initiatives are not only well meaning but much needed and well received. (See Chapter 17.)

Pray, prepare and plan – there are loads of resources in this book to help you prepare your church for HOPE 08 (Chapter 19), to plan your year ahead (Chapter 18), to think about how your young people can get involved (Chapter 9) and to get creatively praying and seeking God about his heart and plans (Chapter 12).

Contact the HOPE 08 office – if we can help you in any way please contact us by email (info@hope08.com), by telephone (01273 571939), or by post (Unit 4, Fairway Business Park, Westergate Road, Brighton, BN2 4JZ).

Watch our website – while we've tried to include as much as possible in this publication, our website www.hope08.com is being constantly updated. There are loads of ideas here but if you have better ones, have learnt from mistakes or have some helpful advice to share please log on to the site and let others know.

CHAPTER 2

WHAT PEOPLE HAVE SAID ABOUT HOPE 08

"

'HOPE 08 provides both a unique and truly significant opportunity to work alongside neighbourhood police officers in improving the quality of life in all our communities. If churches thank and encourage local officers in their day-to-day work and get involved practically in tackling neighbourhood concerns, then the impact could be truly immense.'
Chief Constable Matt Baggot (Leicester) and ACPO Head of Neighbourhood Policing

'HOPE 08 has great potential as a catalyst for grassroots action by local churches, enabling them to engage in sustainable community activity, in other words being and sharing good news!'
Fran Beckett OBE, CEO of Church Urban Fund

'In seeing the many different streams of church networks and denominations united in working together, demonstrating and proclaiming the good news, we are encouraged that this mission dream is becoming a tangible reality. We are more

'HOPE 08 has my unequivocal support.'

than thrilled to be able to stand with others in this kingdom initiative.'
Stuart Bell, Team Leader of Ground Level network of churches

'HOPE 08 will be an excellent opportunity for people of all denominations of the Christian faith to unite in regenerating and transforming their local communities, making them better places to both live and work. HOPE's interaction with Safer Neighbourhood Teams will offer the police, community and faith groups the chance to work together to make their area safer. As with SOULINTHECITY LONDON, HOPE 08 has my full support.'
Sir Ian Blair, Metropolitan Police Commissioner

'HOPE 08 will enable young people to show the generosity of God's love in your locality – and make a difference. I strongly commend it.'
Graham Carter, President of the Methodist Conference

'HOPE 08 will be a wonderful context in which churches can work together to proclaim the Christian gospel in some wonderfully diverse ways. Scripture Union is delighted to be supporting this initiative.'
Keith Civval, Scripture Union

'HOPE 08 is a tremendous catalyst for encouraging and resourcing churches of all traditions to raise their game in community service. It has my unequivocal support.'
Revd David Coffey, President of the World Baptist Alliance and Moderator of the Free Church Council

'As a denomination we are in the midst of our "Catch the vision" process. We are particularly interested in HOPE 08 and its vision of communicating the gospel through words and actions. I am keen to encourage our churches to explore this further.'
Revd David Cornick, General Secretary of the United Reformed Church

'Churches all over Scotland are already involved in a whole host of exciting and innovative mission initiatives – running kids' holiday clubs, social action events, Alpha or Christianity Explored courses, etc. HOPE 08 gives us a unique opportunity to develop this impetus further – calling on churches to work together in outreach and mission in every village, town and city in Scotland.'

David E.P. Currie, Church of Scotland Mission Consultant

'I believe HOPE 08 is a God-given opportunity for the church to work together and share the good news of Jesus in all its fullness. It is a chance to build upon what is already taking place and, working with others, seeing spiritual and social transformation within communities across Scotland.'

Dr Fred Drummond, Scottish Director, Evangelical Alliance

'BRING IT ON!'

'I thank God for the inspiration that has driven HOPE 08.'

'HOPE 08 will be an excellent example of how the UK church is well able to remain locally relevant whilst being nationally coherent. "A million hours of kindness" can be interpreted in so many creative ways; it will be an exhilarating and inspiring year. I am thrilled to be part of such a vibrant, credible presentation of good news.'

Revd Joel Edwards, General Director of Evangelical Alliance

'HOPE 08 is a powerful initiative that, via engagement with the community, expresses the good news of the Gospel in a way that reaches the whole person – body, soul and spirit.'

John Glass, General Superintendent, Elim Churches

'Collaborative and effective mission is at the heart of the vision of Evangelical Alliance Wales, so I am both delighted and privileged to commend highly HOPE 08 as a God-given opportunity to

reach Wales with the good news of Jesus Christ.'
Revd Elfed Godding, General Secretary, Evangelical Alliance Wales

'What a brilliant initiative.'
Pete Greig, founder of 24-7 Prayer

'HOPE 08 is bringing people and churches together, serving God and the local community. It is amazing to see so many people from across the country involved.'
Revd Nicky Gumbel, Holy Trinity Brompton & Alpha International

'The villages, towns and cities of Wales desperately need hope. Young people from churches all over Wales can help bring that hope. We believe that HOPE 08 will build kingdom life here in Wales – we love it, we're excited by it, we'll be part of it, and we're praying that God will use it!'
Nigel James, Development Director, Ignite

'HOPE 08 is a wonderful initiative and demonstration of Christian unity and witness in our society. I pray it will provide numerous opportunities for Christians to engage in the issues that impact the lives of people. It speaks of relevance and making a difference, giving opportunity for Christians to demonstrate the good news where they are. The scope is large, as is the need. May God bless all involved.'
Commissioner Elizabeth Matear, Moderator Elect of the Free Churches

'HOPE 08 is a wonderful opportunity for Christians everywhere, as individuals and as partners, to make a difference in our communities. Whether it be a small act of kindness which brightens someone's day or a group of churches working together to build better communities, the Salvation Army prays that HOPE 08 will help us all to do even more to bring good news and hope into a world which desperately needs it.'
Commissioner John Matear, Territorial Commander of the Salvation Army

'It will be an exhilarating and inspiring year. I am thrilled to be part of such a vibrant, credible presentation of good news.'

'What a brilliant initiative.'

'HOPE 08 is about empowering individuals to make a transforming contribution to society. Keep up the good work!'
Ian Mayer, Jubilee Trust

'I wholeheartedly recommend this grassroots initiative as a way of empowering local churches to be bold in living and proclaiming the gospel in our society. I am particularly delighted that from its beginning HOPE 08 has been an ecumenical initiative which can thus witness to the power of the gospel to unite people in a world of many divisions.'
Cardinal Cormac Murphy-O'Connor, Archbishop of Westminster

'HOPE 08 is an amazing opportunity for Christians across the land to unite, in sharing Christ's love with our nation. Church Army is passionate about reaching out to the least, the last and the lost with the transforming good news of Jesus Christ, and sharing faith through words and action. We are thrilled to be a partner in HOPE 08 and are so excited about what new thing God is going to do among us. Bring it on!'
Mark Russell, Chief Executive of Church Army

'For me, partnership is really at the heart and I want to invite and encourage every person who knows and owns the name of Jesus Christ to become a partner of HOPE.'
Archbishop of York, Most Revd John Sentamu

'HOPE 08 is a wonderful initiative and an opportunity for local churches throughout the country to work in their communities and make a real difference to their neighbours.'
Caroline Spelman MP, Shadow Communities and Local Government Minister

'HOPE 08 represents a remarkable opportunity for the UK Church to 'raise its game' in working with local police, local government and other local organisations to better serve our communities.'
Lord John Stevens, former Commissioner of the Metropolitan Police Service

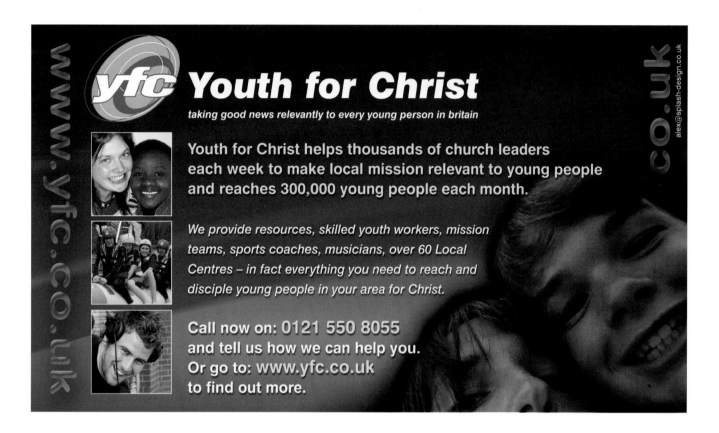
'We are seeing more and more people based in local churches working to make a difference across their communities. I welcome the contribution of HOPE 08. The government is committed to working with faith groups to strengthen community engagement.'
Rt Hon Stephen Timms MP, Chief Secretary of HM Treasury

'An increasingly cynical world will judge us not only by our words but by our deeds. HOPE 08 provides an opportunity for local churches to demonstrate the relevance of the gospel in a

'We love it, we're excited by it, we'll be part of it, and we're praying that God will use it!'

"

very practical way in their local community and can make a real impact. I am delighted to be associated with this venture.'
Steve Webb MP, Liberal Democrat Health Spokesman

'HOPE 08 is a really remarkable vision that has grown out of the success of a number of local urban projects. Christians have to learn how to give an absolutely clear answer to the question, "Why is this good news?"; SOULINTHECITY LONDON and all the related enterprises that have been going on are a wonderful example of how to give such an answer, in terms of the building of responsible, positive communities. Now, with HOPE 08, this vision is being extended, with great boldness, to the whole country – and even more widely. It deserves the warmest welcome. I thank God for the inspiration that has driven it and wish every blessing to all involved.'
Archbishop of Canterbury, Dr Rowan Williams

'HOPE 08 will be a wonderful context in which churches can work together to proclaim the Christian gospel in some wonderfully diverse ways.'

'HOPE 08 is about empowering individuals to make a transforming contribution to society. Keep up the good work!'

CHAPTER 3

WHY BOTHER?

THE THEOLOGY BEHIND HOPE 08

Paul Bayes (Archbishop's Council), Laurence Singlehurst (Cell UK)

GOD'S MISSION AND HOPE 08

The year 2008 is a year of hope, a year of mission. A year when we seek to do more, to do it *together*, and to do it in *word and action*. But most of all, a year when we seek to do mission *in response to the love of God* in Christ Jesus.

WHAT?

We seek to do more because God is always calling his people to press on, to move forward, and to share in his mission. He's not calling us to be frantically busy for its own sake – our mission has to be rooted in the peace and grace of God. But Paul was not ashamed to tell the Philippians '...there is *one thing I always do. Forgetting the past and straining towards what is ahead, I keep trying to reach the goal and get the prize for which God called me through Christ to the life above*' (Phil. 3:13,14, NCV, my italics).

In 2008, we pray that the Lord will give his church that hunger to press forward,

> Some Christians give their main energies to the preaching of the gospel, and others to social action and involvement. But for Jesus Christ there was no distinction.

and joyfully to use our creativity and our energy to do more where we are, so that his kingdom may come more fully.

As we respond to the call of God to do more, the HOPE 08 vision calls us to act as Christians together. Again, this is not something we do for the sake of it. Jesus' prayer in John 17 is 'I pray that they can be one. As you are in me and I am in you, I pray that they can also be one in us. *Then the world will believe that you sent me*' (v. 21, NCV, my italics). Christian unity flows from obedience to God's mission, not out of our own guilt or from the decisions of our committees. As we listen to our own community in 2008, and begin to discern the work God wants us to do there, so we will see that other Christians are God's gift to us for the furtherance of his mission. We will need the love God has given them, if God's purpose in our village, town or city is to be fulfilled: 'I showed them what you are like, and I will show them again. Then they will have the same love that you have for me, and I will live in them' (Jn. 17:26, NCV).

And we're called to do mission *in word and action*. Indeed, this is one way the Lord will draw his people together. Some Christians give their main energies to the preaching of the gospel, and others to social action and involvement. But for Jesus Christ there was no distinction. When Luke wants to remind Theophilus what Jesus was, at the beginning of Acts, he says '...I wrote ... about everything Jesus began to *do and teach* until the day he was taken up into heaven ...' (Acts 1:1,2, NCV, my italics).

This book is full of ideas for the proclamation of the gospel, and for serving people where they are with the practical love of Jesus. Unless we hold these things together – unless we *do and teach* – then we'll fall short of the mission model of our Lord.

WHY?

Well, OK. Do more, do it together, do it in word and action. That explains *what* we are doing in HOPE 08. But *why* are we doing it?

What's our deepest motivation?

There is no better place for us to draw inspiration than John 3:16: 'For God so loved the world that he gave his one and only son, that whoever believes in him shall not perish but have eternal life.' (NIV)

From this well known and powerful verse we have three simple principles to inspire us in mission. Firstly, 'God so loved the world'. Mission and evangelism is so often seen as an action and we get caught up, sometimes reluctantly, in all sorts of methodology. But real mission begins out of love. God's mission to redeem the world came out of his all-encompassing love so we could say that mission begins with a question: how big are our hearts?

When I (Laurence) was a young man I had an experience that changed my life. I was asked to look after a group of children in the slums of Melbourne, Australia, and I was told that one of them would be very dirty and hard to love. Well, how difficult can that be? I thought to myself. Until this little boy ran towards me to be picked up and then I realised his underwear was soaked in urine, full of human excrement and he smelt so bad I wanted to be ill. Sadly, I could not pick the boy up and I turned my back. That night, as I was very depressed, the leader of our Christian community said to me, 'Loving people is difficult, isn't it?' 'Not difficult,' I replied. 'Impossible.' She took me to a passage of Scripture in 2 Corinthians 5, from verse 14, and showed me three principles. Christ died for all which means that every human has great value, the value of Christ himself; whether we are rich or poor, clean or dirty, we all have the same value. Secondly, 2 Corinthians goes on to say, do not look at people from the outside. We need to catch a glimpse of that value. Thirdly, Christ dying is sacrificial which tells us the nature of real love; it is not a feeling, but a choice.

A few days later I met the little boy again but this time, by the grace of God, armed with many prayers for a bigger heart, I saw the little boy in a whole new way and was able to pick him up. As we start HOPE 08 let us ask God for a big heart.

Real mission begins out of love.

It is not just about telling people the words.

The second principle we see in John 3 is that love is incarnational. God sent his Son and the second aspect of our mission is we have to go in the same way. We have to go out of love, not scalp hunting, not out of a motivation to make our churches bigger but just because we love people. We need to be involved with people in friendship, in deeds and action, in words and, above all, in lifestyle just like Jesus was. These days people are very suspicious of words, sadly. We've grown to distrust people who say, 'I have the truth.' We are looking for reality. So, as we go, as best we can, we need to be real, authentic and make sure we're doing what we're saying. It is this that will make a difference. The people that we go to may have a very negative picture of God and Christians and we want to help them on a journey to change their perception of what God is really like, through changing their perceptions of Christians and the church.

Thirdly, mission is a message. God so loved and sent his Son that we would 'not perish but have eternal life'. The third aspect that we need to think about is, what are we going to say and how are we going to say it? It is perhaps important at this juncture to reflect on some words of Jesus himself who taught a wonderful parable about seeds. In Matthew 13, from verse 18, we are told what the parable of the sower means. In this parable there are four different types of soil: the path which is very hard, the rocky places which have very thin soil, the soil with thorns and lastly the good soil. This parable is about understanding. Jesus tells us that the path means those who understand very little and therefore the word has no impact, whereas the good soil is those who understand. In evangelism our responsibility is to help people understand and this is a journey for them. It is not just about telling people the words. If they don't understand those words because of the language we use or because of the way we say it or because at this point they are not really ready to receive all these words, we are not being helpful.

Some years ago, James Engel devised a scale of one to ten to picture a person on a journey to faith. This is a scale from negative to positive. The negative is how they originally may see God and church and the positive is how they can see God and the church in a new way. So if we meet somebody who is at point one on the scale with a negative picture of God and the church and, through our love and words, they go from point one to point three, we have been involved in mission; this is successful mission. I (Laurence) once met a very clever female journalist on a train who had had very bad experiences of Christianity and she was appalled to think that she was sitting next to a card-carrying preacher/missionary. During our two-hour train journey I listened a lot and said a little and at the end she said to me, 'Laurence, you are the first nice Christian I have ever met.' She did not give her heart to God but she did begin the journey. And, if we find somebody at point eight on the scale who has met many other Christians, and been prayed for many times, we may have the privilege of seeing them give their life to Jesus. The point is not where we meet them, it's that however we help them along the scale, we're engaging in mission.

So what we aim to do in HOPE 08 flows from the love of God and the example of Jesus. And so does our motivation. It begins with a big *heart*, as God himself has. It is *incarnational*, living out our reality as Jesus did, and it is communicating the *message* in a way that people understand.

The message has always been the same. That God loves us and is longing for friendship; that our selfishness and sin has separated us from him. Through Christ, God reaches out to us to bring us back into friendship and intimacy as we seek his help to deal with our selfishness, our principle of self-rule and our desire to live for ourselves.

So there you go. That's the 'what' and the 'why' of sharing in God's mission. Now check out the ideas in this book, which will hopefully point you to the 'how' – how to be God's mission people where you are in 2008.

It begins with a big *heart*, as God himself has. It is *incarnational*, living out our reality as Jesus did, and it is communicating the *message* in a way that people understand.

Hope-filled Prayer

Let's keep prayer at the heart of all we do in 2008, to discover God's heart and to allow him to grow ours. For ideas on how to pray throughout the year, see Chapter 12.

Resources

· Sowing Reaping Keeping, *Laurence Singlehurst*. This book helps the reader explore what it means to love people, to sow seeds of faith, to reap the harvest at the right time and to nurture growing faith. Published by Inter-Varsity Press. £6.99 from www.ivpbooks.com.

· Worship Evangelism Justice, *Mike Pilavachi with Liza Hoeksma*. This book explores the meaning of loving God with all our hearts and loving our neighbours as ourselves, providing practical tips for evangelism and social justice. Published by Survivor. £5.99 from shop.soulsurvivor.com.

· Intelligent Church: A Journey towards Christ-centered Community, *Steve Chalke and Anthony Watkis*. This book seeks to reclaim the true heartbeat of the church; the passion to save not itself but the world. Rooted in deep theology but highly practical this book gives you vision of a church that equips its members for frontline work. Published by Zondervan. £7.99.

· Freestyle, *Jo Wells and Andy Frost*. A book about radical discipleship, mission and social justice. Published by Authentic Media. £4.99. Read reviews and order from www.sharejesusinternational.com.

· Church on the Edge, *Chris Stoddard and Nick Cuthbert*. Exploring foundational principles of culturally relevant mission, looking at how 22 diverse congregations are making a difference in their own community. A book designed to envision, inspire and encourage anyone who is committed to reaching this generation with the gospel. Published by Authentic Media £8.99 (incl. p&p) from www.run.org.uk.

· RUN – (Reaching the Unchurched Network) is a growing network of churches passionate about mission in contemporary culture. Members of RUN have access to leading edge outreach thinking and up to date ideas, high quality resources and links with churches and ministries across the UK and beyond to benefit from a wide range of experience. Find out more and join RUN (annual subscription £44 for churches or individuals) at www.run.org.uk.

big ideas

'As people enter the New Year, they are often full of hope about what the coming 12 months will hold.'

CHAPTER 4
FRESH HOPE
JANUARY

Matt Bird (Make It Happen),
Laurence Singlehurst (Cell UK)

As people enter the New Year, they are often full of hope about what the coming 12 months will hold. New Years resolutions are part and parcel of the season with people hoping to give something up or to develop new and better habits.

This hunger for change and a new start provides an excellent opportunity for the church to serve. We could have a huge impact if in villages, towns and cities across the UK, churches worked together to provide a range of New Year resolution lifestyle courses. For example one church could run a course on financial freedom for those who have resolved to sort their money out. Another church could run a health and fitness course, because improving in this area is a common New Year goal. Yet another church could run courses focusing on building better relationships and all the churches could join together to promote their activities across the village, town or city where they are taking place.

The purpose of these courses is to bless people, to serve their needs, to build relationships and to find common ground in which Christians and non-Christians can do things together. Courses should be practical and concentrate on the topic advertised, not veer off into an evangelistic talk. This is a great chance to serve people with no strings attached and if they show interest in the church and its activities then there is a whole year's worth of things going on that you will be able to invite them to!

> The purpose of these courses is to bless people, to serve their needs, to build relationships and to find common ground in which Christians and non-Christians can do things together.

Getting going

In the Great Ideas file below there are ideas for five course topics designed to fit with the most popular New Year aspirations.

If Fresh HOPE is something that you want to start your year with then during the course of 2007 talk to your church and community about what they think the needs are. Pray about the vision both personally and corporately, then choose the courses you think will best serve your area and that you have the leadership, time and skill to set up (you may need to join with other churches to provide these resources between you). Towards the end of 2007 begin to publicise the course or courses within the church and get members to invite their friends. You could print a brochure or flyer advertising the courses and giving clear details about what is available and when. (Increase the impact by combining with other churches in your area and advertising all the courses that are running at the same time.) This can then be used to hand out as personal invitations or could be given to people on the street or at your Christmas events.

GREAT IDEAS AND RESOURCES

1. Health and fitness – a lifestyle course for those who want to lose a bit of weight and/or live a healthier lifestyle.

- **How about a weekly session learning to cook healthy food?** You could use something like Rosemary Conley's *Step By Step Low Fat Cookbook* or check out more health and fitness ideas at www.rosemary-conley.co.uk.
- **Walking is a great way to start exercising;** it has many health benefits while allowing people to go at their own pace and is great for building relationships. If you'd like to

start a weekend walking club visit www.whi.org.uk to find out about walks in your area plus lots of useful information including training for walk leaders.

• **For youth groups,** a sports initiative could be a great way to get active and to bring new people into the group. You could try Youth for Christ's 'Kick Academy' courses; ten-week programmes teaching the gospel and life skills through football. For more information go to www.yfc.co.uk/kickacademy.

• **Start a weight loss programme** at your church such as WeightWatchers – see www.weightwatchers.co.uk/about.

• **If you're using the New Year** as an opportunity to get sporty, you could benefit from the Christians in Sport resources. They support Christians who *Pray* for their friends, *Play* on and off the sports field in a way that honours God and then look to *Say* something of their faith in Jesus. Find out more and check out the free study guides, talks and other resources at www.christiansinsport.org.uk/downloads/index.htm.

2. *Work and vocation* – a lifestyle course for those who want to do something about their work or the way they work.

• **'The Heart of Success'** is a DVD and workbook by Rob Parsons which will enable individuals to explore the best way to find that illusive balance between life and work. Visit Care for the Family at www.careforthefamily.org.uk/hope (for Scotland www.careforthefamily.org.uk/scotland and for Northern Ireland www.careforthefamily.org.uk/ni).

• *Love Work Live Life* – a book by David Oliver about how to discover your work and career as your God-given vocation. Available from Care For the Family, details as above.

You may be able to find some good secular time-management courses too – always popular with today's busy lifestyles!

Walking is a great way to start exercising; it has many health benefits while allowing people to go at their own pace and is great for building relationships.

For youth groups, a sports initiative could be a great way to get active and to bring new people into the group.

3. *Family and relationships* – a lifestyle course for those who want to build better relationships with family and friends.

• **'21st Century Marriage'** and '21st Century Parents' DVDs. Popular speaker and author Rob Parsons explores the joys and challenges of family life in easy-to-view sections – designed to encourage thought and discussion through accompanying workbooks – from Care for the Family, details as before.

• **Connect 2** – a six-part course for newly married couples that has been used across the UK and abroad, which helps those in the early years of marriage address issues of communication, conflict, expectations and intimacy. It also includes marriage preparation for those seeking to make this lifelong commitment – visit Care for the Family, details as before.

• **Family Time** is a ten-session course on parenting and family life for those with young children. The course covers areas like the impact of marriage on family life, communication, how to handle other things that influence children such as TV, computer games, school friends etc.; family values and discipline. All the material you need to run a course is available in the *Family*

Time book and you can buy additional resources at www.new-wine.org, by calling 020 8799 3778 or by emailing info@new-wine.org. New Wine also run regular training courses for those wishing to run the course. Five DVD set with leader's guide is £75.

• *Family Ministry Manual:* A practical guide for every church seeking to address the needs of families in their surrounding communities. Written for church leaders by church leaders it addresses the common issues and challenges that leaders might experience as they seek to impact their communities from Care for the Family, details as before.

• **Parentplay** is a fun seven-week parenting course by Rachel Bright and Rachel Murrill which includes small group discussions, followed by a messy-play time with the children. It focuses on the needs of children and is committed to seeing family relationships develop. Its core value is that healthy relationships are key to children's healthy growth and development. This parenting course both encourages and challenges parents and has a large emphasis on play, hence making it a lot of fun. It is accessible to the abilities and needs of all parents with children under five. Available as a book for £19.99 from www.authenticmedia.co.uk.

• **Parentalk Parenting Course** is suitable for all ages including those who are expecting children. The course is split into eight sections of 20-minute videos which are flexible in terms of how much or little you choose to use. Suitable for expectant parents through to those with teenage children, the videos feature Rob Parsons, Steve Chalke and Dr Caroline Dickinson. Available with a video, leader's guide, activity sheet and magazines to aid completion of the course for £49.95 (plus £2.50 p&p) from www.parentalk.org.uk.

• **Romance Academy** is a sex and relationship education programme (as seen on BBC 2) run specifically for teens that has an excellent format and content that could

> How to handle... things that influence children such as TV, computer games, school friends... family values and discipline.

be ideal for your youth group and their friends. See www.romanceacademy.org for more details.

• **The Marriage Preparation Course** (for engaged couples) and The Marriage Course (for couples who have been married for any length of time) by Holy Trinity Brompton are for any couple that wants to develop or build strong foundations for a healthy marriage that will last a lifetime. Full information and resources for running a course are available from http://themarriagecourse.org and http://themarriagecourse.org/preparation.

• **'The Sixty Minute Marriage'** and 'The Sixty Minute Parent' are available as DVDs and videos with accompanying workbook and books addressing the big questions in marriage and parenthood – from Care for the Family, details as before.

• **Marriage God's Way** is a course that can be used by individuals, groups and couples interested in exploring the biblical view of marriage and addressing the biggest challenges relationships face. The pack features two DVDs, audiocassette and one workbook from Selwyn Hughes. £39.95 from www.cwrstore.org.uk.

Further reading

• *The Highway Code for Marriage*, Michael and Hilary Perrott. This best-selling book is for anyone who is about to get married, thinking of giving up on their marriage or wanting to make their marriage even better. £6.99 from www.cwrstore.org.uk.

• *The Highway Code for Parenting*, Michael and Hilary Perrott. This guide for parents deals with the big picture: love and self-esteem, discipline, character development and equipping children for life. It's suitable for Christian and non-Christian alike, and will be welcomed by anyone about to become a parent, feeling overwhelmed, or wanting to enjoy family life more. £6.99 from www.cwrstore.org.uk.

• *Look before you leap* and *Till death us do part* both by J John are two key books about making marriage work. £6.99 each or £9.98 for both. www.philotrust.com

• *Marriage as God Intended*, Selwyn Hughes. Drawing on his many years of experience as a counsellor and husband, Selwyn blends biblical principles with practical suggestions on how to let God keep your marriage at its best. £6.99 from www.cwrstore.org.uk.

4. Financial Freedom – a lifestyle course for those who would like financial freedom from shopping, debt and the desire for more.

• **The Money Secret Adult Education Course** – designed to provide realistic and

Poverty and Homelessness Action Week takes place from 28 January to 3 February 2008 to encourage churches to find out the needs in their community and think about how they can respond. Find out more at www.housingjustice.org.uk and www.church-poverty.org.uk. For more detail on training around this initiative contact the HOPE 08 office on 01273 571939 or email info@hope08.com.

grounded advice about finance and debt which will not only improve the lives of many families, but will also proactively reduce relationship, marriage and family break-ups. Available as a book, CD and a workbook from www.careforthefamily.org.uk/hope (for Scotland www.careforthefamily.org.uk/scotland and for Northern Ireland www.careforthefamily.org.uk/ni).

Useful reading: *Your Money and Your Life*, Keith Tondeur. Published by Triangle. An in-depth look at all biblical teaching on money issues and their practical outworking. This is also available as a course looking at money and possessions, budgeting, giving, saving, debt, work and family and ethical considerations. See www.creditaction.org.uk for more details and to download self-help guides, money saving tips and information sheets.

www.moneybasics.co.uk is a useful website produced in partnership with Credit Action,

Consumer Credit Counselling Service and GE Money. Contains useful information on handling money and dealing with debt.

5. Kicking It – a lifestyle course for those with a habit that they want to get rid of, perhaps smoking, gossiping, being negative or placing too much emphasis on material goods.

• **Local secular organisations** may be able to help you find good ways of supporting people in kicking these habits; for example try your Primary Care Trust (or Local Health board in Wales) for information about giving up smoking.

Hope-filled Prayer

Make some time and space at the start of 2008 to commit the year ahead to God. Ask him what he would like you to be involved in, pray for the initiatives your church and the churches around you are running.

Christian Unity Week happens 18–25 January and is a great chance to commit to the unity that is at the heart of HOPE 08. See the Churches Together in Britain and Ireland website (www.ctbi.org. uk) for the 2008 theme and to download prayers. For more prayer ideas for January and throughout 2008 see Chapter 12.

Care for the Family are running a number of events to help churches reach out to their community and help people with the issues they face in their lives. You can download a PDF about the event at www. careforthefamily. org.uk/hope.

Family Time course

We felt really blessed having done the Family Time course. It enabled us to have an evening together for ten weeks, discussing the importance of our family that was a blessing and really strengthened our marriage.

The course opened up loads of opportunity for discussion about the history of our respective families, for example the traditions and habits we had brought with us from our own childhoods and those little family habits we wanted to include in our own family to give us our own identity. Each week we were able to think about direction for our family, finding a vision for how we would like it to be and where we were heading, spending more time together, having fun, making memories, helping, sharing, being there for one another.

We started to have family time each week – a time when we can get together and talk about what is going on in our lives, when the children let us know what is going on at school with friends, teachers and so on, and we can bring up things that are worrying or annoying us. Our girls really enjoy this time and even the baby adds his babbling and gurgles!

We even started to make prayers and Bible stories at bedtime a regular thing and try to pick a story that reflects what has been going on during the day or week to reinforce our chats.

We came away with a real feeling of peace, that we were actually doing an OK job as parents and that although there were things we felt we needed to change, we felt reassured that the things we were doing were OK.

(From a couple who did the course.)

'HOPE 08 will enable young people to show the generosity of God's love in your locality – and make a difference.'

'HOPE 08 has great potential as a catalyst for grassroots action by local churches, enabling then to engage in sustainable community activity, in other words being and sharing good news!'

CHAPTER 5

THE BIG HOPE

EASTER

Roy Crowne (Youth for Christ)

Easter is a key time in the church calendar but often means nothing more to those in our community than a break from school or work and a time to eat a lot of chocolate. The Big HOPE is all about making Easter more accessible to those outside church and exploring both sides of the story of Jesus' death and resurrection. There is time over Easter to focus on the sorrow of Jesus' suffering on the cross, a theme that allows us to reach out to those around us who are in pain themselves. It also provides us with a wonderful opportunity to gather the church and the community together to celebrate Jesus' resurrection and the new life we find in him. Easter gives us time to bless and serve our communities and to get across the important message of the cross in fresh and interesting ways.

Easter provides us with a wonderful opportunity to gather the church and the community together to celebrate Jesus' resurrection and the new life we find in him.

GREAT IDEAS

There are loads of ways to celebrate Easter in your village, town or city and all these ideas can be adapted to suit your area and the resources available to you. It may be a great chance to empower your young people to take a lead in the planning.

There are of course sensitivities around the timings of these events (for example some churches would not choose to hold a celebration event until after Easter Sunday) so make sure you choose a time that fits with your tradition and that of those around you.

1. Fun day

One great way to have a positive impact on the community is to create a funfair festival feel around the positive points of Easter, based in a local shopping centre, school or community centre. You could even have it outside if the weather is good! This is a great chance to work with all the churches in your area to provide a really creative fun day, full of hope, life and chocolates.

Again depending on your tradition this could take place on Palm Sunday, the Saturday in the middle of Easter, over the Easter weekend or on Bank Holiday Monday.

- **Create a running programme** of activities and games, with moments within the programme where the crowd can gather to watch a focus presentation such as a four-part passion play or other elements of the Easter story, performed by local children.

- **Run Easter-themed ideas** such as games, treasure hunts, music, songs, karaoke, message boards, a chocolate fountain, bouncy castles, face-painting, stalls; give away bulbs to be planted, have an Easter bunny in costume to give out eggs and give opportunity and resources for people to make Easter cards. Think about how fun day activities can be adapted for the Easter theme such as having graffiti boards that contain both dark and light areas that invite people to communicate about the contrasting sides of pain and joy in life.

• **Brand items** such as T-shirts, bags and gifts with the HOPE 08 logo and slogan to make it clear what the fun day is all about (see www.hope08.com to get the HOPE 08 logo).

• **Hold a Swap Shop** where people promise services to their community.

• **Hold a balloon release** with a message of hope.

• **Provide an area** where people can be quiet and spend time reflecting with a prayer wall or a place where they can light a candle. You could also put out a prayer box for people to leave their prayer requests.

• **Organise a treasure hunt** by bike, car or foot.

2. Lost

Between the cross and the resurrection, the disciples did not know what was happening and were in a time of great confusion and pain. Perhaps during Lent or on 'Holy' Saturday you could hold an event in your church that marks this period of mourning and reaches out to those in the community currently suffering bereavement. Possible elements could include the following.

• **A service of reflection or prayer** could be provided for those who have been bereaved in the previous 12 months. Invite all the family and friends of those who have died and read out the names of their loved ones who have passed away.

• **The day could focus on** a sense of loss with the opportunity to explore issues of broken relationships, divorce, illness, disease, despair, debt, cancer etc. It should offer a sense of direction and destiny through the loss, and discuss how death is a part of life that needs to be addressed.

• **There could be prayers** and the opportunity to light candles – for example, a town could light one thousand candles.

• **There is often interest** in the community about different elements of spirituality so you could hold a night looking at a subject like angels

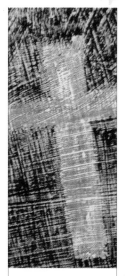

A service of reflection or prayer could be provided for those who have been bereaved in the previous 12 months.

or the concept of heaven. Explore the questions of 'What's out there?' and 'How do we connect with it?' as well as offering prayer. More details are available at www.hope08.com.

• **Find out about funerals** that are happening on that day and send flowers from the churches in the community.

• **You could link the day** to environmental issues and look at the death of the planet and our responsibility to take care of it. For inspiration visit www.ecocongregation.org for England and Wales; www.ecocongregationireland.org for Ireland and www.ecocongregation.org/scotland for Scotland.

3. The Last Supper

The Last Supper is a key element in the Easter story and meals have a very important place in family and community life. You could maximise this in a number of creative ways, getting groups together to share food and to show the love of Christ.

• **You could start with a meal** as a family round a table, recognising that a family is core to community.

• **Every cell or small group** could run a remembrance meal with monologues, poetry or humorous anecdotes.

• **If there is** homelessness in your area, offer your services at a local project addressing the issue. Many organisations value teams coming in to cook a meal for shelter residents or serve food and drinks at drop-in centres.

• **The food could include** the meats, herbs, breads and wine used in the Passover meal, each carrying its own significance and telling the story of Easter.

• **Alternatively, small groups** could run a themed dinner party based around the story of Jesus and his twelve disciples. Find out more at www.hope08.com.

• **Just as Jesus washed** the feet of his disciples, we can think about how we can serve those in our community who serve us. For example invite key agencies like the emergency services, teachers etc. to a special restaurant meal to say thank you, offer to pray for them and bless them for their work.

Other ideas

- **Donate Easter eggs** to groups of children in the local community, particularly those in hospital or living in difficult circumstances or give the eggs to those in your church to take into school with them. They could present the true meaning of Easter to their friends and then give out the eggs.
- **Think of practical ways to serve** those around you such as washing your neighbours' cars just to bless them. Chapter 6 has loads of ideas for ways you can get practical in your community.
- **Invite friends round to watch a film** such as *The Passion of the Christ* or Agape's *Jesus* film (for children you could use the *Chronicles of Narnia* film instead). Alternatively get hold of Bible Society's *Reel Issues* magazine that will help you discuss the spiritual elements of current cinema releases or J John and Mark Stibbe's *Passion for the Movies* book which looks at spiritual messages behind popular films such as the *Godfather* trilogy, *The Lord of the Rings*, *Bridget Jones's Diary* and *Finding Nemo*.
- **Offer local radio stations** a short interview or story showing what Easter is about and/or what your church is doing in the local community to celebrate.
- **Link up with another church** in your area that holds a Stations of the Cross service and invite your church members and community to attend. If you hold such a service yourself, invite others to attend.
- **Hold a flower festival** or decorate all the visible crosses on local churches with flowers on Easter Sunday.
- **Run a photo club** around the theme of Easter.

Take a group to the HOPE 08 evangelistic tour on the theme of the cross and resurrection or get trained to deliver this in your area. This high impact fast-paced multimedia event run by Youth for Christ and The Message Trust will communicate the good news of Jesus in a suitable way for young people using the theme of hope. Find out more about the tour at www.hope08.com

- **Perform a passion play** (see Resources for more detail).
- **Work in your local school** to hold assemblies or take lessons about what we're celebrating at Easter – see Chapter 10.
- **Public foot washing** can be a way of showing that the church wants to serve the community.
- **Because of what Jesus did on the cross** we moved into a 'new age'. Redeem this term from its current meaning and hold a 'new age' party celebrating our new life in Jesus.
- **Do a gardening makeover** for any council waste ground, plant a cross in the garden when it's done.
- **Prison Fellowship:** Use the fact that Jesus was imprisoned to reach out to those in prisons near you. This needs to be considered and well-planned so contact the chaplain at a nearby prison and check out www.prisonfellowship.org.uk (England and Wales) or www.pfi.org (Northern Ireland and Scotland) to see how you can help.
- **In the run-up to Easter,** schools could be invited to prepare for Easter through writing prayers for themselves, their school, family and community. Read these prayers at your Easter Sunday service and invite the children and their parents.

Hope-filled Prayer

The forty days of Lent can be a great time to pray for your community, and any events that you are organising or taking part in over Easter.

If you've not already started a prayer triplet, why not do that around Easter and keep it going at least until September? Three people gather together regularly to pray for three friends each who aren't yet Christians. Find out more and see further prayer ideas in Chapter 12.

RESOURCES

You'll find more information about getting started with many of these ideas at www.hope08.com. Other resources that might be helpful are:

Environment

· For more information on environmental issues such as climate change see the Campaigning section of www.tearfund.org.

Evangelistic resources to give away

· Easter SONrise is an evangelistic resource explaining the truth and significance of Easter as well as outlining the history of many Easter traditions. Price £1.99 single copy, prices reduced for bulk buy – visit www.philotrust.com for more detail and to order.

· What is a Real Christian?, Luis Palau. Luis Palau presents the basics of the gospel in straightforward language. He explodes many common myths about what makes a Christian before going on to reveal the truth – and the steps people need to take in order to become children of God. Pack of 6, £4.99, individual copies, 99p. Order from www.cwrstore.org.uk.

Film

· Reel Issues – Bible Society monthly magazine that gives you stimulating material to talk about the latest must-see films in the light of the Bible. To subscribe visit www.biblesociety.org.uk –

Use the fact that Jesus was imprisoned to reach out to those in prisons near you. This needs to be considered and well-planned so contact the chaplain at a nearby prison

£21 for 12-month subscription (monthly issues are accessed online). For Scottish Bible Society resources see www.scottishbiblesociety.org. For resources from Bible Society in Northern Ireland see www.bsni.co.uk.

· At www.agape.org.uk/store you will find a number of versions of the Jesus film including resources for small groups and schools.

· Passion for the Movies, J John and Mark Stibbe, £8.99 from www.philotrust.com.

General

· For Easter resources to use with your youth group, go to www.lifewords-global.com/easter.

· www.rejesus.co.uk/easter have many Easter-themed resources, see their website for more details.

· 'Easter SONrise' DVD: A live-recording of J John speaking at Hillsong London explaining the truth and significance of Easter. £9.99 from www.philotrust.com. Accompanying booklet £1.99 or from 45p if you bulk buy.

· Easter Cracked is full of ideas for Easter celebrations, evangelistic outreach for the whole family, craft, drama and events. There are ideas for all-age events for Passover and Good Friday plus assembly outlines and ideas for working with youth and the under five age group. £9.99 from www.scriptureunion.org.uk. For resources from Scripture Union Scotland see www.suscotland.org.uk, for Scripture Union Northern Ireland see www.suni.co.uk.

· Celebrating the seder, Nick Fawcett. This book teaches Christians about the Jewish Passover tradition and enables you to hold your own seder meal. With extensive background information, a guide to the Hebrew terms, a section of recipes, a list of useful websites and practical advice and guidance at every stage. £12.99 from www.kevinmayhew.com.

· CPO (Christian Publishing & Outreach) produces a wide range of posters, banners, invitation cards, booklets, tracts and other outreach resources specifically themed for use at

HELP!

We can help you prepare for mission through listening to God and understanding his Word / equip your church with resources and training / serve your community in word and action

mission: we can do it together

See more online:
www.scriptureunion.org.uk/hope2008

Scripture union

Easter and will have specific HOPE 08 resources available from www.cpo.org.uk/hope08. A team of outreach advisors are available on 01903 263354 to help suggest the most appropriate resources for local needs.

Grief

A Grief Observed, C.S. Lewis. Published by Zondervan. £6.99 from www.wesleyowen.com.

When Life is Changed Forever, Rick Taylor, www.careforthefamily.org.uk/hope (for Scotland www.careforthefamily.org.uk/scotland, for Northern Ireland www.careforthefamily.org.uk/ni).

Help my kids are hurting, Marv Penner. Published by Zondervan. £4.99 from www.wesleyowen.com.

Lent

· **Just Church** from Church Action Against Poverty is a course that could be used at Lent which helps churches focus on what they can

If you've not already started a prayer triplet, why not do that around Easter and keep it going at least until September?

do practically to engage with social justice and poverty issues around them. The course is split into ten to 12 modules that can be run over any time period, or sections can be chosen that are of particular interest to the group. Find out more at www.church-poverty.org.uk.

· **Life Source** is a five-session course on prayer for Lent by Robert Warren and Kate Bruce encouraging a discovery of new-found joy and delight in prayer for novices and old hands alike. The course combines Bible study and discussion with a creative, hands-on exploration of five prayer patterns drawn from our rich Christian heritage. £3.99 from www.chpublishing.co.uk.

Passion plays

· **Saltmine** have passion plays that are fast moving and easy to perform. See www.saltmine.org for more details.

CHAPTER 6

HOPE ON THE STREETS

MAY BANK HOLIDAY / PENTECOST

Dan Etheridge
(Soul Survivor and Soul Action)

May Day Bank Holiday weekend: 2–5 May 2008

As we move into the Pentecost season we remember when the Holy Spirit first came on the members of the early church. They spilled out of the room where they had been meeting and praying together and their actions were seen by the thousands gathered in Jerusalem, ultimately seeing 3,000 people saved. This is a great reminder to us to let our activities break out of our church buildings and to get onto the streets where we live.

One of the challenges for HOPE 08 is to get Christians all over the country joining together to give one million hours of kindness in the form of practical help to their communities. The long Bank Holiday weekend in May (the weekend before Pentecost) provides us with a great opportunity to serve the spiritual, physical and social needs of those around us and to get really practical! Each hour we give to serve others is an hour where we are worshipping God by following the example Jesus set for us in being the gospel as well as talking about it.

Each hour we give to serve others is an hour where we are worshipping God by following the example Jesus set for us in being the gospel as well as talking about it.

You can use the HOPE on the Streets high point to launch some longer-term community work (Poverty Action Week can help you plan and prepare for this, see www.faithworks.info) or to celebrate what you already do in your community, depending on where your church is at. Whatever you do, the aim is that relationships are built, people's needs are met and the church is engaged with its community.

Below we've outlined what a weekend could look like but the ideas can be adapted to suit any needs and resources, and can work just as well run by a small church group as undertaken by churches across a city.

Mornings

Taking time out to worship, learn and pray together is a great way to start the day as it sets the tone for the project and helps us to remember this service is all part of our worship to God. It's a good opportunity to learn more about God's heart for us to go out and serve those around us with unconditional love and to get envisioned for the tasks ahead.

Afternoons

This is when the projects are carried out and you get stuck in with the practical work. See the Great Ideas section for inspiration for what you could be getting up to – anything from gardening to portable nail bars have been tried!

Don't forget to keep praying – either have a prayer team who go around and pray for each project or ask a number of teams to take ten minutes out of each hour to pray.

Evenings

It's good to have a social activity during the evenings to bring people together and have some fun. Depending on the size of your group and your resources this could be anything from a casual meal at someone's house; a prayer meeting; social time together as a team; an outreach café; a gig or even a citywide evening celebration.

GREAT IDEAS

Any attempt to serve a community needs to be well planned and thought through. Although we want to respond to God's Spirit and prompting and serve spontaneously as part of our lifestyle, we also want our concentrated efforts to be well thought through, well planned and effective at achieving our aims. Good intentions often only get us so far! **Check out Chapter 17: 'Engaging with your community' to find out how to go about assessing and responding to the real needs of your town.**

It's important to think through what your aims are and what resources you have at your disposal before committing to projects because you don't want to start something you don't have the time, skills, money or people-power to finish. There are hundreds of ideas for projects so resources shouldn't count anyone out from taking part in HOPE on the Streets – for example you don't need any money to drop into sheltered housing and speak to the elderly people there and you can distribute food to those in need easily through www.fareshare.org.uk.

In the past, specific types of projects have proved to be really successful at capturing a community's imagination:

Whatever you do, the aim is that relationships are built, people's needs are met and the church is engaged with its community.

There are hundreds of ideas for projects so resources shouldn't count anyone out from taking part in HOPE on the Streets

- **Visual projects:** Initiatives that make a real visual difference to a community both during and after completion are really effective, such as cleaning graffiti from stairwells and removing rubbish from local parks.
- **Interactive projects:** Projects that look to involve local people have been some of the most successful in various recent missions. Whether it be a community clear-up or a parent and toddler scheme, these projects get volunteers and residents alongside each other, talking about the local area and giving people in the community the incentive to get involved in making a difference in their own streets and estates.
- **Established projects:** Many projects that are part of the longer-term work of the church in the community are really beneficial to support as are those set up by any local charity. These projects, from youth clubs, holiday events and regular community action initiatives, are likely to be thankful for some extra pairs of hands and will have ways of working that volunteers can easily fit into. If we don't pay attention to existing initiatives there is a risk that we will reinvent them and potentially damage both our credibility and the work of the existing project at the same time.
- **Evening events:** Evenings are a great chance to host events that convey the gospel message through performance, teaching and testimony. These events could include barbecues, cafés, youth events, music performances and even nail bars all of which are fun and a real blessing to the community. Some of the best and most successful ideas allow volunteers to spend time socialising with local people, chatting to them about what is going on and why.

The following ideas and events have been undertaken all over the country, but obviously you'll need to research the needs and interests of your own community before setting up or planning any specific projects yourself. The 'Soul Action GO: LOCAL' CD Rom (see Resources) is a great resource to get you started.

Gardening projects
Tidying the village green
Clearing up parkland
Painting fences/gates
Making window boxes
Helping the elderly with overgrown gardens

Projects on estates
Graffiti removal
Clearing alleyways
Cleaning stairwells
Cleaning lifts
Litter picks
Painting murals
Painting railings

Home projects
House clearance
Decorating
Building furniture
DIY-related help

Kids/youth work
Summer play clubs
Sports events
Cafés
Fun days

Events
Community barbecues
Music concerts
Nail bars/Beauty salons
Street performance

Sports competitions
Clubs and dinners for the elderly
DJ/Dance/Performing Arts workshops

And loads more...
Perhaps hold your church service outside on the Sunday and then start a community barbecue straight afterwards.

Log your hours of kindness at www.hope08.com so we can hit our target of one million across the UK!

Think how many lives could be saved if we all used one of our hours of kindness to donate blood. Find out where you can give locally at the following websites
www.blood.co.uk
(England and North Wales)
www.scotblood.co.uk (Scotland)
www.nibts.org (Northern Ireland)
www.welsh-blood.org.uk
(South, Mid and West parts of Wales)

Don't forget to link your church plans for Rogation community walks and village food events to your HOPE 08 plans

Organisations that can help
Besom
Besom is an organisation that can help you make a difference no matter how much time, money, skill or resources you have at your disposal. It started in the London area but now there are many Besom's all over the country – check out their website for one near you and to find out more at www.besom.com.
You can give:

- **Your time** – as an individual or with a group undertaking activities from sorting through donated goods to picking up and delivering items in a van to those in need.
- **Your skills** – can you cook, paint, teach, do DIY or carpentry? Whatever your skills, Besom can put you in touch with someone who will benefit from what you have to offer.
- **Your goods** – give Besom things you no longer need like baby equipment, linen, curtains, clothing, crockery or toys and they will make sure they're given to people who really need them.

Faithworks
Faithworks is a movement of thousands of individuals, churches and organisations motivated by their Christian faith to serve the needs of their local communities and positively influence society as a whole.

RECOMMENDED RESOURCES

Unwrapping The Gift — Encouraging the local church to pray — John Preston — 978-1-85078-582-8 £3.50

THE BOOK OF Y — PETER MEADOWS JOSEPH STEINBERG — 978-1-86024-568-8 £7.99

HOW TO BE HEARD IN A NOISY WORLD — CHURCH PUBLICITY MADE EASY — PHIL CREIGHTON — 978-1-85078-716-7 £8.99

Parentplay — A 7-week parenting course for parents of children under 5 — Rachel Murrill and Rachel Bright — 978-1-86024-592-3 £19.99

BREAKING NEWS... — TODAY :: A PRACTICAL COURSE DESIGNED TO HELP YOU SHARE GOD'S GOOD NEWS TODAY :: A — J.JOHN — 978-1-86024-549-7 £4.99

You can join the Faithworks network as an individual member or as an affiliate church and access a library of information, training and resources to support you in your community work.

See www.faithworks.info for more details and to sign up (free to individuals, £20 annual subscription for churches and organisations).

Share Jesus International are working with other Christian organisations to develop a new event as part of HOPE 08 from 9 –11 May. For further information see www.pentecostfestival.co.uk.

Volunteer Bureaux

There are volunteer bureaux across the country that can put you in touch with a range of organisations that would value your help.

Try www.timebank.org.uk, the Scottish Council for Voluntary Organisations www.scvo.org.uk, Northern Ireland Council for Voluntary Action (NICVA) www.nicva.org, Wales Council for Voluntary Action (WCVA) www.wcva.org.uk or Volunteer Development Agency www.volunteering-ni.org.

Getting started

- **Think through the needs** in your community and the resources your church has available.
- **Hold an evening, day or weekend** of prayer in preparation for the activities about three weeks beforehand.
- **Decide whether you will run your own project**, join with other churches or work with established projects and charities.
- **Assign a co-ordinator** to lead the activity.
- **Get church members to sign up** for the weekend in advance so you know how much people-power you have and therefore how many projects you can commit to.
- **Keep a track of all the hours** given and log them on www.hope08.com.

The Noise provided ways to connect with individuals, families and many community groups in ways that haven't been possible before.

Hope-filled Prayer

Global Day of Prayer – Pentecost Sunday 11 May 2008.

This will be the fourth Global Day of Prayer and will see millions of Christians in around two hundred nations around the world taking part in ten days of prayer leading up to Pentecost. On the Sunday afternoon, venues large and small will hold prayer gatherings after which groups will spend ninety days blessing others. To find out how to link in as a local church or larger group visit www.globaldayofprayer.co.uk.

Making a noise in Gloucester
Joe Knight

The Noise in Gloucester drew young people from twenty churches over a weekend in July to serve and practically help people in many communities across the city with the love of Jesus Christ.

The whole project spanned a weekend packed with worship, prayer, servant-hearted activities and community events whereby young people were united, encouraged in their faith and communities impacted with the good news – and seven people became Christians.

What happened?

We started with a worship celebration on the Friday night and continued to learn more about the heart behind the project on the Saturday morning. During the afternoon, teams of young people travelled across the city to various 'zones' to paint, litter-pick and clear rubbish away with a focus to love and serve others with their actions. The projects we took on came from working with local residents during the weeks and months of preparation before the weekend.

To add to this, 'connect teams' travelled around the various zones carrying out surveys among the local communities. They explained what was happening to those who didn't know and also invited people to a community event that evening.

We had three evening events in different parts of Gloucester to continue the momentum of what had happened during the day. Community barbecues, café nights, sports and youth club activities all played a part in making an exciting evening accessible to local people. We also had space for youth to give testimonies and for everyone to hear an evangelistic message before we finished.

Gloucester Cathedral became home for a 24-7 style prayer room from the Friday all through to Monday. Young and old made use of the space for three days to let prayer and action work together. We kept up to date with what was happening and the prayer room definitely helped give a focus that loving God means loving our neighbour as the Bible tells us.

With a passion to worship God in every area of our lives, The Noise has really helped break down barriers among Christian youth and has provided ways to connect with individuals, families and many community groups in ways that haven't been possible before.

Since this project happened, the adults in our church have increasingly got behind this initiative so this year we're planning to have a month of 24-7 prayer followed by an intergenerational Noise project. As always we're trying to see how these events fit into the day to day life of our communities, so we're finding ways to stay in touch with community groups, to be involved and always available to help so the impact of these larger events is not forgotten.

RESOURCES

- **GO:LOCAL** CD Rom from Soul Action. This CD Rom gives you loads of practical advice about doing Jesus-centred community work. See www.soulaction.org for more detail.

Books

- **Express Community**, by Phil Bowyer, is an inspirational and practical guide to give young people the methods and principles needed for social action. Suitable for youth, student and young adult groups, plus teachers and schools workers this book shows how evangelism and social action are inextricably linked. £7.99 from http://youth.tearfund.org.

- **Everybody Wants to Change the World,** Tony Campolo. More than a hundred practical ideas for compassionately responding to the needs of others. Including suggestions about working with those in poverty, honouring and assisting the elderly; helping immigrants assimilate and supporting the sick; respecting and serving the disabled, showing compassion to those in prison, and caring for the environment.

A leader's guide makes this adaptable for group study, as well as individual reading. £10.49 from www.equippingthechurch.co.uk.

· **Building a Better World: Faith at work for change in society**, Malcolm Duncan. This book invites anyone who longs for a fairer world to consider whether commitment to justice could be strengthened by Christian spirituality. £7.99 from www.faithworks.info.

· **What can one person do?** Edited by Sabina Alkire and Edmund Newell. Is the problem of poverty too much for individuals, churches and communities to tackle? This book offers practical suggestions for real things we can do in our personal lives to bring the vision of a world without poverty a step closer. £12.95 from www.dltbooks.com.

General

· **See www.soulaction.org** for more information on 'Noise' weekends and to download helpful resources such as consent and volunteer application forms.

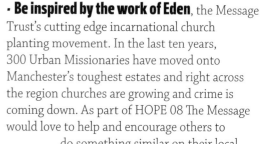

Is the problem of poverty too much for individuals, churches and communities to tackle?

· **Be inspired by the work of Eden**, the Message Trust's cutting edge incarnational church planting movement. In the last ten years, 300 Urban Missionaries have moved onto Manchester's toughest estates and right across the region churches are growing and crime is coming down. As part of HOPE 08 The Message would love to help and encourage others to do something similar on their local deprived estates. If you would like help, advice, or resources contact eden@message.org.uk.

· **In Wales, GWEINI** (the council for the Christian voluntary sector in Wales) provides an umbrella organisation and resources for churches who want to get involved in longer term community projects. See www.gweini.org.uk and the book *The Naked Church* for more detail (published by GWEINI, £6.50 incl. p&p.)

CHAPTER 7

HOPE EXPLORED

SEPTEMBER

Steve Clifford
(Pioneer Inspire/ Soul Survivor)

Over the course of the summer, loads of activities have been happening in thousands of churches with fun days, festivals, arts and music academies and kids clubs. Relationships have been built and contacts have been made. Since Easter, prayer triplets have been meeting on a regular basis praying for specific individuals. Now imagine for a moment that all over the country in all kinds of different settings and to all kinds of different people an invitation goes out. 'How about exploring the Christian Faith?'; 'Would you like to know more about Jesus?' The invitations are extended via text, email, postcards in the local shop and doctor's surgery, on notice boards in the leisure centre, on billboards, radio programmes and cinema adverts – some are big and impersonal, others very specific, extended face to face, friend to friend through the contacts made over the summer.

In September 2008, there will be a national Alpha initiative advertising the Alpha course on billboards, in cinemas, in regional press and on radio, on buses and in taxis. This annual national initiative coincides with hundreds of regional and local publicity campaigns run by churches to raise the profile of Alpha as a way for people to explore the Christian faith. This is underpinned by the Alpha prayer initiative which encourages special prayer events in local communities.

Many people have questions about the Christian faith and courses like Alpha give them an opportunity to hear a bit more about it and discuss their views in a relaxed and non-threatening environment. Meeting together each week allows for those on Alpha courses to feel they are part of the community of the church and are welcomed in no matter where they are at in their spiritual walk.

Many people have questions about the Christian faith and courses like Alpha give them an opportunity to hear a bit more about it and discuss their views in a relaxed and non-threatening environment.

GREAT IDEAS

Alpha has been hugely successful around the world, seeing many come to faith but it is not the only way of running such a course. HOPE Explored can and will express itself in all kinds of different ways and can be adapted for many different circumstances. However the common elements that have proved effective and therefore should be included are:

- **A relaxed and informal atmosphere**, perhaps aided by refreshments or a meal.
- **An encouragement for conversation** where there is no pressure to have to agree, but a genuine opportunity to engage in an exploration of the Christian faith.
- **These conversations are open to all** – whether they have faith or not.

Alpha has provided a wonderful contribution to the church not only in the UK but all over the world. Alpha's profile will be high during the September Alpha campaign which adds credibility to your own local invitation programme. But there are also other resources available and in some settings, individuals and churches will make use of these rather than Alpha, such as Back to Church Sunday (www.backtochurch.co.uk) – see the Further Resources section for more details.

So what are the settings in which Christianity could be explored?

1. In universities and colleges

Student Alpha, Fusion (an organisation working with students across the UK) and Soul Survivor are rising to the challenge of inviting every 'Fresher' to a Student Alpha course during the Freshers week of 2008.

2. Schools

Youth Alpha working in partnership with Youth for Christ are making available a wonderful resource, whether delivered during school lessons, lunchtime or after-school clubs. Aimed at the eleven to eighteen age group, wouldn't it be wonderful to see Youth Alpha in hundreds if not thousands of schools during the September period?

> There is no pressure to have to agree, but a genuine opportunity to engage in an exploration of the Christian faith.

> *Wouldn't it be wonderful to see Youth Alpha in hundreds if not thousands of schools during the September period?*

3. The workplace

Workplaces come in all kinds of shapes and sizes. In some there is a canteen/restaurant, in others that's a thing of the past. A number of courses within the Resources section could well be adapted for a short lunchtime session or an after-work get-together.

4. Sports club/leisure centre

How about extending an invitation to your football team, rugby club or dance class to explore Christianity? It might be after a training session; it might be on a separate night. It could involve Alpha or one of the other courses, or might simply be about sharing your own faith and giving people an opportunity to discuss it. Or you could book one of the YFC teams to run a course that uses sport as an opportunity to learn more about Christian values. See Resources for more details.

5. Your street/neighbourhood

Maybe you have lived on your street for years, chatted over the garden fence, had an occasional barbecue or just exchanged Christmas cards – but now there is an opportunity to do more. How about a specific invitation to explore Christianity through running an Alpha-style course on your street?

6. At the pub or in Starbucks

Pubs and coffee shops are places where people feel comfortable and relaxed, making them a great setting for interesting discussion. Maybe send a

specific invitation to a small group of friends and use some of the courses and resources available to enable you to explore the Christian faith or to talk about Scripture.

7. The pre-natal group/play group/ nursery group

You get together for coffee already – how about extending an invitation to watch an Alpha or NOOMA DVD (see Resources) together and discuss? The NOOMA DVDs are also particularly good for young people.

8. Churches

Many churches already run courses so let's not forget them in our plans for 2008! Let's make them strategically co-ordinated with our other activities and prayer-filled to make the most of the year of HOPE.

9. Youth group

Get your youth group to text and email their friends inviting them to come for pizza and to go through the Youth Alpha material aimed specifically at eleven- to eighteen-year-olds.

10. Book club

Book groups are still very popular so if you regularly meet up with friends to discuss what you've been reading, how about suggesting a book like J John's *The Life* and discuss a few chapters each night? (Published by Authentic Media. £3.99 from www.philotrust.com.) Or try *Dinner with a Perfect Stranger*, a novel by David Gregory about a modern-day meeting with Jesus, £5.99 from www.hodderchristianbooks.co.uk.

11. Story-telling evening

Get someone with a great story which is personal, relevant and glorifies God to tell their tale (either in a home or down the pub – wherever would work best) and then, with a group of friends, open up the discussion and talk about it.

12. Film night

Watching a film can be the perfect way to spend time with friends. Why not hire *The Passion of the Christ*, invite a few people to come and watch it and then open up the conversation? Alternatively get hold of Bible Society's *Reel Issues* magazine that

Get your youth group to text and email their friends inviting them to come for pizza and to go through the Youth Alpha material.

will help you discuss the spiritual elements of current cinema releases or J John and Mark Stibbe's *Passion for the Movies* book which looks at spiritual messages behind popular films such as the Godfather trilogy, *The Lord of the Rings*, *Bridget Jones's Diary* and *Finding Nemo*.

Getting started

- **Having read our ideas**, what do you think would suit the people in your church and area? Pray about what may be suitable.
- **Would your congregation need training** to be able to deliver the activity? If so, check out the training resources and make sure teams are trained well in advance of September.
- **Build the course or activity** into your church outreach strategy; think about advertising and financial support that it may need to succeed.
- **Think about how you will disciple** new people who come to faith through the activity such as through the Beta course (www.beta-course.org).

Harvest is a great time to celebrate local produce, farming, gardens and people's creativity and is the second most popular time for people to go to church in rural areas (after Christmas). Use your church's Harvest Festival activities to reach out to your community and provide a focus for your HOPE 08 ideas.

Hope-filled Prayer

Why not combine a prayer walk with a leaflet drop for a course your church is running? See Chapter 12 for more details plus lots of other prayer ideas.

CASE STUDY

A testimony from Alpha

Jamie Hinde's first lucky break as an actor came at age eighteen, when he was cast in an exciting role for the Royal Shakespeare Company. The good acting jobs continued and later he went on to produce and direct as well. But something inside him was dissatisfied, which led him to embark on a spiritual search.

'I read about Buddhism, Taoism, etc. ... Then I got a very good part in *The Lion King*, in London. I remember one night playing Scar [the evil lion] in front of 2,500 people and standing there thinking, 'I don't feel anything...' The buzz had gone. So eventually I left – I felt there was something else...

'Soon after, my girlfriend encouraged me to do an Alpha course at HTB. When I started it I was in a bad way. I was drifting, with no real zest for anything. Every cynical bone in my body was going, 'What am I doing here?' Then something amazing happened two weeks into the course. By this stage something in my heart had clicked. I was on a train and I read through the *Why Jesus?* booklet. Then I said the prayer at the end. I had the most amazing, profound experience. I expected nothing – but felt incredible peace, joy and bliss. The Spirit was coming into me, saying, 'Jamie, it's true. Let's go for it.

'Since then I haven't looked back. I've helped on other Alpha courses and I'm at that stage where I'm going, 'OK Lord, use me...'

'Every cynical bone in my body was going, 'What am I doing here?' Then something amazing happened two weeks into the course.'

RESOURCES

Evangelistic courses and resources

1. Alpha

The Alpha course is a practical introduction to the Christian faith, designed primarily for non-churchgoers and new Christians. Alpha aims to present the core truths of the Christian faith around which Christians of every denomination can unite.

The course is normally run over a period of ten weeks with a weekend or day away halfway through. A typical evening consists of supper, followed by a short time of worship, a talk that can be given live or shown on DVD/VHS and, after the talk, coffee and small-group discussion. Over the ten-week course, 15 topics are addressed such as 'Who is Jesus?' and 'How can we have faith?' and 'Is there more to life than this?'

If you would like to find out more or to come along to be trained on how to run an Alpha course, please see www.alpha.org for details on an Alpha conference or a local Saturday Equip and Refresh training day near you.

Youth Alpha

Youth Alpha is low-key, friendly and fun. It runs on the same basis as Alpha but is tailored to the eleven-to eighteen-year-old age group.
See www.youthalpha.org.

Alpha for Students

Based on the Alpha material but aimed at students, the course has taken place on campus, in student houses, in churches, at pubs, in cafés and even in McDonald's! See www.alpha.org/students.

Alpha in the Workplace

Designed to fit into busy working schedules, Alpha in the Workplace sessions tend to be shorter than other Alpha meetings and do not include worship times. They tend to take place in lunch hours or even over breakfast and give opportunity for you to engage in meaningful dialogue with your colleagues. See www.alpha.org/workplace.

(You can also find out about *Alpha in Prisons, Alpha in a Catholic Context, Senior Alpha* and *Alpha for Forces* at www.alpha.org.)

2. Christianity Explored

This ten-week course (with a weekend away part way through) explores who Jesus was, what his aims were and what it means to follow him. It is suitable for those looking to understand more about the Christian faith or as a refresher course for those within the church. You can use the materials provided to do the talks yourself or buy the DVDs to show if you would prefer. Full resources are also available to help you run the course including a leader's manual, study guides and promotional materials.

Find out more and purchase resources at www.christianityexplored.com.

3. Y Course

The Y Course has eight sessions that explore life's big issues. Each talk is available on DVD, is introduced by Steve Chalke, then speakers from Joel Edwards to Jeff Lucas explore questions like 'Can anyone really know what God is like?' and 'Who wants to be stuck with a bunch of boring old rules?' The DVD also comes with a CD Rom including a Course Leader's Handbook, Group Leader's Guide and Participant Notes. Other materials such as invitation flyers and videos can also be purchased. *Beyond Belief (Y Course)* by Peter Meadows and Joseph Steinberg is available in paperback for £6.99 from www.authenticmedia.co.uk.

Y Course materials are available from major Christian retail outlets and websites.

4. Emmaus: The Way of Faith

Emmaus is a course designed to welcome people into the Christian faith and life of the church, by teaching the basics of Christianity and developing the discipleship of maturer Christians. It is rooted in Jesus' model of evangelism, nurture and discipleship demonstrated in the story of the Emmaus Road. First it encourages evangelism in

Alpha in the Workplace sessions tend to take place in lunch hours or even over breakfast and give opportunity for you to engage in meaningful dialogue with your colleagues.

the local church and provides practical advice on developing contact with those outside of church. The core material is aimed at enquirers, new Christians and those looking for a refresher course and covers the basics of Christian life. The final stage is about deepening an understanding of Christian living and discipleship.

There is also a Youth Emmaus course for those aged eleven to sixteen.

Find out more and purchase supporting resources for both Emmaus and Youth Emmaus at www.e-mmaus.org.uk.

5. ReJesus

ReJesus is a website that was created for individuals and churches to share information about Jesus with those who don't know much about him. Using a website allows people to discover more about the things that interest them, at their own pace. The site is split into five sections which cover the story of Jesus and some of his most famous followers, how Jesus is alive today and how we can meet him, provides simple suggestions for reflection and prayer, allows people to explore different expressions of Jesus in art and poetry, plus there is opportunity for online discussion.

Visitors can sign up for a free eight-week course (sent via email) that explores 'Developing Happiness' and there are lots of links that can be emailed to interested friends.
See www.rejesus.co.uk for more details.

6. Lyfe Course (Bible Society)

Lyfe is a course designed to help people encounter the Bible and what it has to say about their everyday lives. Small groups meet together regularly, generally in public places like coffee shops and restaurants. They take a passage of Scripture and then discuss what it tells them about God, how it relates to life today and how they can apply the verses practically. Lyfe is accessible to everyone, even those who aren't Christian, and gives time to read, reflect and respond to God's word. Find out more and download your free welcome pack at www.lyfe.org.uk.

7. NOOMA DVD (Zondervan)

NOOMA is about providing spiritual direction in a way that is accessible to people as and when they need it using the popular format of short films available on DVD. Each film comes with a discussion booklet, and topics covered include the meaning of love, suffering and trusting God. See www.nooma.com for more details. DVDs can be ordered from UK Christian bookshop websites.

8. CaFE

Catholic Faith Exploration is a video-based programme that can be used in churches, schools, colleges and prisons. It is designed to run in four short modules which fit into school terms and aims to get people excited about their faith, provide an

Lyfe is accessible to everyone, even those who aren't Christian, and gives time to read, reflect and respond to God's Word.

opportunity for good community and empower people to share the good news with those around them. Supporting video materials are available. See www.faithcafe.org for more details.

9. TEN – J John

TEN is a DVD series exploring the relevance of the Bible message today. Each of the ten 45-minute programmes features vox pops, interviews and J John's compelling explanation for the relevance of a commandment God gave us. The sessions highlight the modern need for these timeless truths, for example using the commandment 'Thou shalt not commit adultery' to discuss how to affair-proof your relationship. The box set comes with a user guide to explain how to make the most of the course and provides pointers for further discussion.

See www.philotrust.com for more details and to order resources (£29.99 for the DVD boxset).

10. Youth For Christ sports teams

YFC has a number of mission teams who are available to come alongside churches and schools to run high-profile, professional courses that provoke thought in young people. The courses aim to develop their physical, moral, spiritual and social values and include a Kick Football team, a Fly Basketball team and a Skate team, all of which provide an educational and challenging experience. See www.yfc.co.uk/teams for more details and to book.

11. The Essence Course

The Essence Course aims to provide a way for the church to reach out to those who are currently seeking their own spiritual truth in New Age activities and elsewhere. Held in a neutral environment (e.g. a pub, library or gym) the course runs over a six-week period or as a residential weekend and provides an experiential introduction to the Christian Faith – www.sharejesusinternational.com.

12. Start!

Start! By Robin Gamble is a six-session basic introduction to the Christian faith which assumes no previous knowledge and is often used pre-Alpha. The sessions use a mix of videos, time to chat, discussion activities and time for reflection in a down to earth way. It is designed to help people think about where they are going in their lives, to discover the good news of Jesus and to decide how they want to respond.

Available from CPAS for £39.95. Tel: 01926 458458, www.cpas.org.uk.

FURTHER RESOURCES

- **Back to Church Sunday** is a Church of England initiative to provide a warm welcome to anyone who hasn't been to church in a while as well as those who have never been. This can be

Christian Enquiry Agency

The Christian Enquiry Agency aim to make it as easy as possible for people to find out about the Christian faith. Working nationally and in partnership with all of the major mission organisations, they provide a central point of enquiry and supply information in confidence and free of charge. They also offer follow-up services and support and can put enquirers in touch with their local church when they are ready. You can add their contact details to any of your materials and if people get in touch they will receive high quality, contemporary materials (print, DVD or via the internet) free of charge.

CEA can be contacted in the following ways:
By post: FREEPOST MORE HOPE
Email: more@morehope.info or more@christianity.org.uk
Internet: www.morehope.info, www.christianity.org.uk or www.rejesus.co.uk/hope
SMS: text HOPE to 81025

linked to Harvest or run as a separate event and resources are available (such as T-shirts, prayer cards and posters) to help you advertise the day effectively. In 2008 Back to Church Sunday is on 28 September.
See www.backtochurch.co.uk for more details and to order resources.

- **Christians in Sport** provide plenty of talks and documents you can download aimed at people investigating Christianity. See the Investigating Christianity section at www.christiansinsport.org.uk.

- **Reel Issues** from Bible Society, £21 for 12-month subscription (monthly issues are accessed on line) see www.biblesociety.org.uk. For Scottish Bible Society resources see www.scottishbiblesociety.org. For resources from Bible Society in Northern Ireland see www.bsni.co.uk.

- **Passion for the Movies**, J John and Mark Stibbe, £8.99 from www.philotrust.com.

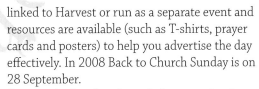

CHAPTER 8
THE GIFT OF HOPE
CHRISTMAS

Andy Hawthorne (The Message)

In 1999, we reached our low watermark as a church when only around 35 per cent of the UK population attended church over the Christmas period. Since then the numbers have been steadily increasing, particularly in the last couple of years. In 2006 the Daily Mail reported a Church of England statistic that 43 per cent of the population were planning to attend a church that Christmas. This means that around 27 million people came through the doors of our churches that Christmas; a huge opportunity to relevantly share the good news of a God who was so desperate to bring us hope that he left heaven and came to earth.

Through the Gift of HOPE we want to encourage and resource local churches to take what they already do well and see if they can make it even better but we also desire that these churches look beyond their services and plan to reach out in word and action over the festive period in numerous creative ways; through community action, local radio, care for those living in poverty and much, much more.

> We want to encourage and resource local churches to take what they already do well and see if they can make it even better.

GREAT IDEAS

- **Work with other churches in your area** to offer a free Christmas wrapping service in your local shopping centre. In the run up to Christmas get your church to donate gift wrap and ribbons and sign up to a timeslot to wrap presents. The impact of offering a free service that takes the stress out of Christmas shopping prompts people to ask 'Why?' You don't need to launch into great theology of grace and giving but can say that you just want to bless people. Have invitations to local church Christmas services available.

- **Work with Social Services** to find young people in your area who will not be receiving many presents this Christmas. Get your church to bring unwrapped presents to church in November/start of December that would be suitable for the age groups Social Services suggest. Discuss with Social Services the best way to distribute the gifts.

- **Take your Christmas carols out of the church** and into your local supermarket, shopping centre, hospital or old people's home. Again, don't collect money, just bless people with the festive music, hand out Christmas goodies like mince pies, and invite people to your Christmas carol services.

- **Work in your local school** taking lessons or running assemblies that explore the story and themes of Christmas. See Chapter 10 for more detail on schools work.

- **Liaise with the police** to close off a high street for a few hours one evening (say 5.30–8.30 p.m.) to have a fun open-

> Work in your local school taking lessons or running assemblies that explore the story and themes of Christmas.

air Christmas event. Work with local traders and see whether they would like to stay open, provide mulled wine and mince pies, place Nativity displays in shop windows, have a band and/or carol singers – you could even run your own stall with homemade cards and gifts from your church members.

- **Find new and creative ways to retell the Christmas story** – inside and outside the church walls. Organisations such as Lifewords can help you bring the biblical story to life through a number of resources designed to tell the story through written words and drama. Lifewords provides adaptable resources (print, film, web, graphics) to help you take the story to public spaces and community places. Take Lifewords to schools, to markets, to pubs, or offer places of prayer and reflection in the middle of the great Christmas shopping rush. Download and order resources, share ideas, and steal other people's at www.lifewords.info/christmas.

- **Christmas services:** Christmas carol services should be a welcoming and non-threatening environment for people who don't usually come to church. Think about how you can make your service more accessible such as

  1. Inviting local schools to bring their choirs to sing at the service. Many proud parents would love to come to see them.

  2. Having mince pies and mulled wine after the service to give a chance for your church to meet visitors.

  3. Providing a welcome pack for visitors which could include information about your church and your services the rest of the year; give away booklets and DVDs such as those listed in the Resources section.

  4. Having a team of people looking out for visitors so they can

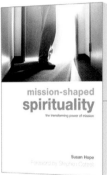

Emmaus: The Way of Faith is a course designed to welcome people into the Christian faith. Going beyond the basics in an engaging and interactive way it can be used with small groups to nurture new believers and encourage ongoing Christian discipleship with more mature Christians. Visit *www.e-mmaus.org.uk* for more details.

Mission-shaped Spirituality
The transforming power of mission
Sue Hope
£7.99   *978 07151 4080 2*   *A5*   *160 pages*

If your shelves are overloaded with books on how to *do* mission, create some space to engage with this book. No to-do lists. No win-win strategies. Instead this discerning book reflects on the inner resources and attitude of mind required to engage in mission in a post-modern, pluralist society.

Fresh Expressions
Skater church...cell church...messy church...All over the country Christians are beginning new initiatives to connect with those who are currently outside church. These DVDs give you an excellent window on what's going on around the country

expressions: the dvd 1
stories of church for a changing culture
£12. 99 978 07151 4095 6
Running time 100 minutes
Directed by Norman Ivison
Presented by Diane Louise Jordan

This DVD includes 14 stories of fresh expressions that are happening around the country.

expressions: the dvd 2
changing church in every place
£14.99   978 07151 4128 1
Running time 108 minutes
Directed by Norman Ivison
Presented by Diane Louise Jordan

This DVD focuses on four specific areas where fresh expressions of church are breaking new ground: work & leisure, rural, sacramental and youth. Also includes six discussion starters.

MAKING CONNECTIONS
PRACTICAL AND REFLECTIVE RESOURCES FOR MISSION AND EVANGELISM

CHURCH HOUSE PUBLISHING   For more details visit www.chpublishing.co.uk

quickly welcome them and find them a seat plus people to talk to.

5. Providing details of and invites to any courses you are running that may be of interest, such as your next Alpha-style course or a Fresh HOPE initiative

• **Sing Christmas:** There's a really simple way you could get people in pubs, community centres, residential homes, hospitals and prisons listening to and celebrating the real meaning of Christmas. How? Follow the example of churches in Leicestershire by working with a local radio station to broadcast a live interactive carol service to the community. Venues throughout the county are invited to Sing Christmas by joining in with the service broadcast live from a pub by BBC Radio Leicester. The BBC website lists the venues taking part as well as providing carol sheets that can be downloaded and photocopied. See www. bbc.co.uk/leicester/faith/features.

The service itself is interactive – everyone is invited to sing along with the carols and take part in activities such as decorating a tree, sharing chocolate, pulling crackers, lighting a candle and hugging a neighbour! Here are some comments following the 2006 broadcast:

'Sing Christmas brought many people into our café – around fifty took part.'

> Christmas carol services should be a welcoming and non-threatening environment for people who don't usually come to church.

> *Broadcast a live interactive carol service to the community.*

'Brilliant. Lovely. Was like having a church in our own front room. Residents loved it.'

'Sing Christmas brought together the largest group of villagers for years. Around ninety people packed into The Dog and Gun.'

Sing Christmas is organised by the CHAD Churches' Media Trust for Leicestershire with help from Churches Together in Leicestershire, in partnership with the BBC.

This great idea could be easily replicated in your area by working with your local radio stations, either the BBC or one of the growing number of small independent community stations. Your church could even apply for a licence to run your very own local station over Christmas.

To find out more about Sing Christmas, contact Jeff Bonser at jeff@singchristmas.org. uk. For details of independent community radio stations and licences contact Jonathan. Bellamy@crossrhythms.co.uk.

• **Use the Churches Advertising Network (CAN):** The Churches Advertising Network (CAN) is an independent, ecumenical group of Christian communicators which exists to provide high quality national Christian advertising campaigns, especially around major festivals, and to provide the means for local churches to share in and receive the benefit of such national campaigns. Find out more at www.churchads.org.uk.

• **Radio HOPE** – supported by Cross Rhythms: Christmas is a great time to offer interesting and creative radio broadcasts and to tell your community more about HOPE 08. See Chapter 16 for more detail on how you can work with Cross Rhythms to produce a month's worth of radio broadcasts. You could also work with Cross Rhythms to produce adverts about your HOPE 08 campaign. Contact info@hope08.com for more details.

• **Angels down your street?** Would you like to find a way of engaging your local council, planners, businesses and schools in a conversation around the gospel story? What if that discussion could find artistic expression across your community? Christmas can give you just such a platform and Bible Society has experience on cultural engagement that might help you get started. Last year, working with world-class designers Kite Related Design, Bible Society worked to develop new and innovative Christmas decorations for Swindon, where the society is based. Working together with local authorities, business and communities they created unique moving angels to be part of the town's Christmas decorations. Up to four metres wide, these giant angels brought a new focus on the biblical accounts of the Nativity.

You could take this concept for development in your village, town or city, bringing the debate and expression of the Christmas festival to the very people with the position to shape and influence it. There is already the tried and tested angel design that you could use and adapt in discussion with local groups, or you could look to build on this work with new themes that connect directly with the people of the area. We can offer consultancy to get you started and to help put Christmas back into Winterval!

For more information about the work Bible Society did, contact luke.walton@biblesociety. org.uk. For Scottish Bible Society resources, see www.scottishbiblesociety.org. For resources from Bible Society in Northern Ireland, see www.bsni.co.uk.

Getting Started

• **What resources do you have available** to bless your community this Christmas? Get teams of church members to run with the ideas you think are workable and make sure all appropriate external groups are contacted (e.g. Social Services for present giving and shopping centre managers for present wrapping).

• **Think through the ways** you can make your carol service more accessible to people who don't go to church regularly.

• **Pick a Sunday late in November/early December** to talk about spreading hope around the world (see below).

We can offer consultancy to get you started and to help put Christmas back into Winterval!

Ideas for spreading HOPE around the world

• **Samaritan's Purse**. In previous years close to one million people in the UK have filled a shoe box with gifts for children in need so why not invite your local community to take part? Bring hope to children and offer your community a way to show compassion and generosity to children all over the world who are victims of war, poverty, famine, disease and natural disaster while sharing the good news of Jesus Christ. Your church can host an Operation Christmas Child-themed National Shoe Box Sunday using resources from Samaritan's Purse. Find out more and download resources that you can tailor for a Shoe Box Sunday at your church including presentations, talk notes, prayers and interactive activities from www.samaritanspurse.uk.com. Boxes are dropped off at local collection points.

• **Compassion.** Christmas is a great time to not only bring hope to your community but to reach out to other parts of the world. Have you wondered how your church can make an impact on world poverty? By partnering with Compassion to change the lives of individual children your church can do just that. Compassion seeks out some of the world's most vulnerable children and

Putting churches at the heart of the community

MILLIONS OF CHILDREN AROUND THE WORLD ARE VICTIMS OF WAR, POVERTY, FAMINE AND DISEASE. THROUGH A SIMPLE GIFT FILLED SHOE BOX, CHILDREN IN THE UK SPREAD LAUGHTER AND HOPE TO CHILDREN LIVING IN POVERTY.

HOW YOUR CHURCH CAN GET INVOLVED

▸ENCOURAGE YOUR CONGREGATION
to do shoe boxes, order leaflets that explain the project and get going!

▸REACH OUT TO YOUR NEIGHBOURS
by inviting community members to pack a shoe box and attend a Shoe Box Sunday Service.

▸OPEN THE DOORS OF YOUR CHURCH
to the public by becoming a Drop Off Point where boxes are collected.

▸BECOME A SHOE BOX PROCESSING CENTRE
where volunteers from all walks of life work alongside volunteers from your congregation.

WHAT'S IN THE BOX FOR THE LOCAL CHURCH?

▸CONNECT WITH THE COMMUNITY
Congregations invite their communities to join them in doing shoe boxes. Rev. David Newton from Clayton Baptist said: "We invited 700 people to a shoe box service, 25 people from the community came and 6 people continue to come to our church! It is a unique, non-threatening way of reaching out!"

▸EVERYBODY CAN DO SOMETHING
There are lots of different things to do! From packing a shoe box and knitting scarves to shopping, driving vans around to collect boxes, to sorting boxes in the warehouse…

▸YET ANOTHER JOB FOR THE MINISTER? NO, NOT AT ALL!
Enthusiasm for the project creates its own momentum. It usually takes only one keen member to bring the congregation on board.

COLLEGES
CLUBS
SCOUTS AND BROWNIES
WOMENS GROUPS
YOUTH ORGANISATIONS
LOCAL BUSINESSES
SCHOOLS
FAMILIES

VISIT OUR WEBSITE TO SEE THE OPERATION CHRISTMAS CHILD VIDEO WITH STORIES OF CHILDREN RECIVING GIFT FILLED SHOE BOXES!

To order your free resources visit:
www.samaritanspurse.uk.com or call: **0870 011 2002**

Samaritan's Purse
INTERNATIONAL RELIEF

'It is a fantastic way for churches and communities to pull together and get involved with something that makes a real difference to the lives of those in need.'

JOEL EDWARDS
General Director Evangelical Alliance

Samaritan's Purse International Ltd., Victoria House, Victoria Road, Buckhurst Hill, Essex, IG9 5EX **telephone** 0870 870 8333 **Email** info@samaritans-purse.org.uk **www.** samaritanspurse.uk.com   Samaritan's Purse registered as a charity, number 1001349

with the help of individual sponsors provides them with the skills and opportunities they need to change their lives and the lives of those around them. Working exclusively through local churches in developing countries, Compassion ensures that there is financial integrity, long-term commitment and the opportunity for every child to hear and respond to the good news of Jesus Christ. To find out more about the work of Compassion and how your church can get involved visit www.compassionuk.org or call their church engagement specialist on 01932 836490. See the Case Study for inspiration on how you can start to change the world.

Hope-filled Prayer

In the run up to this time of celebration, why not hold a Thanksgiving dinner? Invite friends and family round for a meal to share stories, pray and worship.

You could also hold a week of 24-7 prayer in preparation for your Christmas carol service. See Chapter 12 for more details and lots of other prayer ideas.

CASE STUDY

Give the Gift of HOPE this Christmas
Kate Smith, Compassion UK

Many of us feel that as Christians we are called to make a difference in the world and to reach out to those who live in poverty. It is easy to become overwhelmed when we hear that over half of the children in the world today live in abject poverty and that each day another 30,000 die from easily preventable causes but if every member of the body of Christ can help even just one person, we will be playing a valuable role in the kingdom of God.

> **Together the church has established a child development programme where the neediest children in the community are provided with basic health, nutrition and educational support in a Christian context.**

'I used to hide criminals in my home, run gambling tables, and push illegal drugs,' said Nang Maising, a fifty-year-old grandmother who lives in Lorega in Cebu City, the Philippines. At first glance Lorega is full of death, pain and darkness, as it is located in the centre of the city cemetery with tarpaulins draped between the tombs, creating dark alleyways. The only sounds of hope are the cheerful squeals of small children who scamper between the broken headstones playing hide-and-seek. With the help of sponsors across the world, the Cebu City Alliance Church is nurturing the new life that these children possess.

Historically, the Lorega community was policed by local gang members and drug dealers, but now an alternative set of leaders is finding its way into positions of influence, thanks to the Alliance Church. Individual Christian sponsors have given the church the financial resources and support to reach their people with the message of hope.

Together the church has established a child development programme where the neediest children in the community are provided with basic health, nutrition and educational support in a Christian context.

Keen to find out about this alternative way of living, parents of children who attend the project have flooded to the church. Through those parents, gambling dens have been torn down and drug rackets disbanded and a day care centre built. This rejuvenation could never have taken place without the commitment from Compassion sponsors across the world. Working together as the body of Christ, Christians in the Philippines and Christians across the world are bringing the light of Christ to those in need.

If your church would like to learn more about sponsoring a child or a number of children in a community visit www.compassionuk.org.

RESOURCES

Evangelistic resources to give away

• **'More to Christmas'** DVDs from Viz-a-Viz come gift-wrapped and contain stories of 11 people for whom Jesus is making a real difference in their lives. At just £2 a copy this is an affordable and quality evangelistic tool, also available as a magazine for £1.
See www.vizaviz.org.uk for more details and to order.

• **More than a Christmas Carol, It's a Wonderful Life** and **What's the point of Christmas?** are all booklets produced by J John's Philo Trust exploring themes of Christmas using well-known Christmas films and traditions. Single copies £1.99, bulk buy from 45p per copy, www.philotrust.com.

• **God With Us** from Lifewords is a slim publication telling the Christmas story in the Bible's own words suitable to give away at services and events. There is space to write your own message or to add your church details and can be given away as a Christmas card.
See www.lifewords.info/christmas.

Events

• **More to Christmas Event:** More to Christmas is a professionally produced, entertaining and thought-provoking multimedia event ideal for Christians and non-Christians. Viz-a-Viz will provide speakers, hosts and a theatre group to perform as well as multimedia material for this two-hour production. An ideal opportunity to work with other churches in your area to hire a neutral venue such as a school hall or theatre for around five hundred to a thousand

Work with other churches in your area to hire a neutral venue such as a school hall or theatre for around five hundred to a thousand people.

Find out more about holding an Advent Light Relay at www. hope08.com

people. To find out more and discuss costs, contact Viz-a-Viz via their website www.vizaviz.org.uk/moretochristmasevent.htm or by calling 01268 530531.

General

• **Lifewords:** creative resources for faith-centred living: Lifewords is an international mission agency that exists to connect people with the Bible and to each other – and to experience the relationship with the God that it speaks about. They produce creative, meaningful ways to help people connect to the Bible's life words as an essential part of everyday life and worship as individuals, and as a church.

Their range of booklets, toolkits, and new media resources help tell the Bible's story and involve others in the conversation. All Lifewords materials are designed for you to use and adapt to connect life words in your own culture, in your own world, in your own way. Order, download, share ideas, and join the conversation at www.lifewords.info/christmas.

• **CPO (Christian Publishing & Outreach)** produces a wide range of posters, banners, invitation cards, booklets, tracts and other outreach resources specifically themed for use at Christmas and will have specific HOPE 08 resources available from www.cpo.org.uk/hope08. A team of outreach advisors are available on 01903 263354 to help suggest the most appropriate resources for local needs.

• **www.rejesus.co.uk/christmas** have many Christmas specific resources including an overview of the Christmas story, karaoke carols, nativity puzzles, prayers and meditations and a look at the Father Christmas tradition.

• **Youth for Christ** Christmas resources suitable for your youth group are available free from www.hope08.com.

• **Graham Kendrick** is producing an album for Christmas 2008 with the theme of HOPE 08 in mind. Find out more at www.hope08.com.

• **'Christmas Unwrapped'** DVD: A live recording, J John speaking at Hillsong London unpacking the true meaning of Christmas. Aimed at the unchurched but enjoyable for everyone. £9.99 from www.philotrust.com.

Publications

• *Christmas Wrapped Up* and *Christmas Re-Wrapped* are two publications from Scripture Union that are bursting with ideas for all ages for outreach and celebration at Christmas. Visit www.scriptureunion.org.uk for more detail and to order. For resources from Scripture Union Scotland see www.suscotland.org.uk, for Scripture Union Northern Ireland see www.suni.co.uk.

• *Together for a Season – All-age material for Advent, Christmas and Epiphany,* Gill Ambrose, Peter Craig-Wild, Diane Craven, Mary Hawes. A practical resource book full of creative ideas to transform the seasonal liturgy of Advent, Christmas and Epiphany into a multi-sensory and interactive worship experience for all ages. It includes: fully worked out services, step-by-step instructions on ways to introduce creative elements into services and suggestions on how to use the ideas in group work, homes and outreach activities. £22.50 includes free CD Rom from www.chpublishing.co.uk.

Tackling Poverty

• **Compassion** produces a number of *free* resources to help your church explore their Christian responsibility to those living in poverty. Each resource includes a DVD and Bible study booklet that will help you to get to grips with poverty and how we can make a lasting difference.

1. Hand in Hand. Join Jeff Lucas in Ethiopia to explore how churches are changing lives and shaping futures with the help of Compassion.

2. Bridges of Hope – J John explores how we need to share our faith in word and deed.

Unpack the true meaning of Christmas

3. A Life of Love – Graham Kendrick explains why helping those living in poverty is at the heart of worship.

Find out more about Compassion and order resources free from www.compassionuk.org.

• **Samaritan's Purse:** Sermon outlines, invitations, posters and other ideas for your Shoe Box Sunday, as well as regional contacts and the opportunity to work together with your local Shoe Box community is available on the website: www.samaritanspurse.uk.com. Leaflets on how to pack a shoe box, posters for the campaign, campaign video/DVD can all be ordered from the website as well.

RESOURCES FOR CHILDREN

• *Cool Christmas* is a booklet from J John's Philo Trust helping children aged three to six discover what Christmas is all about. Single copies £1.99, bulk buy from 45p per copy, www.philotrust.com.

• *Christmas Treasures* also by J John is aimed at children aged six to nine exploring the customs and traditions around the festive season. Single copies £1.99, bulk buy from 45p per copy, www.philotrust.com.

Across the UK, people are joining with Oasis to help bring transformation - socially, spiritually, emotionally, physically and environmentally, to local people and communities.

Volunteering with Oasis

Volunteer with Oasis at one of our pioneering community hubs providing a whole range of services to its local community...

Training with Oasis

Train with Oasis and get equipped to help young people make life changing decisions when it matters the most...

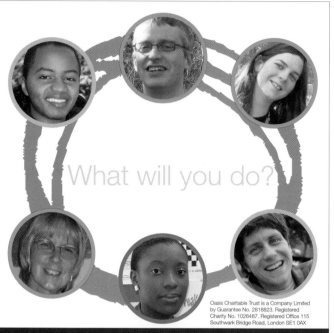

What will you do?

Oasis
for people & community

Visit www.oasisuk.org to find out all you need to know about getting involved!

"**Christians** do not just '**hope**' that the world will be a **better** place; we are **convinced** it will be.
That is why we **do what we do** - and keep doing it."

Malcolm Duncan, Leader of Faithworks

Join with over 20, 000 individuals and churches who are committed to serving the needs of their local communities in order to see society transformed.

By joining the Faithworks Movement today you can access inspirational resources and a host of other practical information to help your church or project engage with its community more effectively.

faithworks

Join today at **www.faithworks.info**

CHAPTER 9

THE HOPE REVOLUTION

SEEDING A YOUTH MOVEMENT

Gavin Calver (Youth for Christ)

The HOPE Revolution is a viral movement of young people who want to have a significant impact in their village, town, city, community or school for Jesus. Young people have the enthusiasm and energy to transform the nation; we need to capture their imaginations, empower and encourage them to see what a huge difference they can make to the world around them.

Historically we've been told that young people are shaped by their genetics and background but Judith Harris (well-known American sociologist) tells us [1] that in fact it is the culture and values of their peers that has the most influence on who and what they become. This provides us with a tremendous challenge and opportunity to reach the young people in our nation by empowering those in our churches to reach out to their friends and peers. If we could empower and equip our young

We want to do everything we can to help them catch the dream and vision to see a HOPE revolution that changes our nation – our part is to serve them to make it happen.

people to live authentic Christian lives in their schools, colleges and in their leisure activities we could help them to start a revolution. We want to do everything we can to help them catch the dream and vision to see a HOPE revolution that changes our nation – our part is to serve them to make it happen.

When Jesus walked the earth leading the greatest revolution of all time, he chose to do it alongside twelve people, some of whom were probably quite young. History has continually proved that young people have frequently spearheaded revolutions – dissatisfied by their surroundings they have found themselves compelled into action. An ever-ageing church in the UK has led us to a time when a revolution is needed to change the world. In 2008 we dream of a generation of young people taking seriously the needs of their world and reaching out together. This revolution will remove organisational and denominational boundaries as evidenced by the range of youth organisations on board including Soul Survivor, Alove, CPAS, The Message, Serious4God, Youth Alpha, Big Ideas, Fusion, Urban Saints, Youth for Christ and Scripture Union.

Who are these young people?

In England, 11 per cent of young people aged eleven to nineteen go to church. [2] If we assume this percentage to be the same in the rest of the United Kingdom then, based upon the various 2001 Census results, this equals a total of over 742,000 young people. [3] The dream is to see 100,000 young people who want to change the world mobilised into action and taking part in this dynamic movement.

Our passion is to release teenagers from being pew-fillers to leading a new breed of missionaries, and to see their friends from outside church finding faith and getting involved too. Lots of young people are already living these kinds of lives but the aim of the revolution is to bring them all together.

Through the Internet, we have the ability to link up young people from wherever they are across the country, providing a support network for those who feel isolated and a feeling of excitement and encouragement to all about activities going on. It's really simple to get involved; to start with encourage your young people to text the word 'hope' to 83010*. They will then receive a text with their very own unique password which they can use to access the HOPE Revolution website: www. hope-revolution.com. The website will have ideas specifically aimed at how they can get involved in all aspects of HOPE and will have a 'revolutionary only' area featuring inspirational ideas and practical advice. In this publication we've also tried to suggest ideas that will appeal to young people but one of the successes of HOPE 08 will lie in groups coming up with their own ideas.

Ideas and stories can be shared through our online MySpace community (www.myspace.com/thehoperevolution). Here we can bring young people together from across the country, building relationships and creating space for creativity and excitement about the things that are happening. In addition, young people can share their YouTube videos and flickr pictures with one another. Monthly stories and updates will also be available via email about what is happening throughout the UK.

The dream is to see 100,000 young people who want to change the world mobilised into action and taking part in this dynamic movement. Our passion is to release teenagers from being pew-fillers to leading a new breed of missionaries.

* text messages cost 25p

We want to spark something that has a significant and lasting effect and the true success of this revolution will be in a lasting radical generation of young people. Such a group will live for Jesus with every sinew of their being for the rest of their lives, in turn encouraging the next generation to live the same way.

There is more information for youth leaders, pastors and parents on the HOPE 08 website www. hope08.com including a list of useful resources for using with young people.

www.hope-revolution.com
www.myspace.com/thehoperevolution

After you've told your young people about HOPE 08, encourage them to take a 'Holy Moment'. Give them an opportunity to stop and think about whether they want to be involved, to bring this commitment before God and to ask him to help them have hearts that are sold out for him and his purposes. When they've made a decision get them to text us to let us know they're on board with the revolution!

GREAT IDEAS
For young people to get involved in HOPE 08

Pass these ideas on to your young people but encourage them to see these as some suggestions and to come up with their own creative ways of bringing HOPE.

- **Make every Friday an AOK day** – log on to www.soulaction.org for weekly suggested Acts of Kindness (AOK).
- **Go into a charity shop** and confuse them with your generosity – offer them more money than they're asking for an item and if they're not happy, offer them more. It's haggling in reverse!
- **Find a local social project** such as a homeless shelter and offer your services for a few hours, a weekend or on an ongoing basis.
- **Make friends with someone** from another culture to your own.
- **If you've enjoyed a TV programme,** call the broadcaster and let them know.
- **Email someone** and tell them why you like them.
- **Organise a group** to pick up litter in your school or on your street.
- **As a youth group** go to your local police station and ask them how you can be praying for them.
- **Look for someone eating alone** at lunchtime and invite them to join you and your friends.
- **Run a course exploring Christianity** in school (See Chapter 10).
- **Join together** with your small group or friends at school and sponsor a child. See www.compassionuk.org.
- **Persuade your family** to change all their light bulbs to energy saving ones – you know it makes sense!

There are loads more ideas throughout this publication and of course on the website but these are just our suggestions – see what your young people can come up with.

Hope-filled Prayer

24-7 has been one of the most exciting prayer movements to happen in years. Get your young people to take the lead, set up a 24-7 prayer room and sign up to hourly slots so that twenty-four hours a day people are praying for the community and the HOPE 08 initiatives you are running.

See www.24-7prayer.com to find out more.

Go into a charity shop and confuse them with your generosity.

Tearfund are launching a new course to help young people connect with God's heart for the poor and to equip them to take action locally and globally. Find out more at www.tearfund.org/youth

RESOURCES

Training and Events

- **Soul Survivor** run five-day events aimed at teenagers and one for students and twenty-somethings (called Momentum). Each conference in 2008 will have a seminar stream dedicated to equipping young people for evangelism and mission. Find out more about Soul Survivor at www.soulsurvivor.com/uk (seminar details will be available nearer the time). Dates for 2008: 18-22 July: Momentum, 11-15 August: Soul Survivor Week A, 16-21 August: Soul Survivor Week B.
- **The Art of Connecting** is a seven-week training course from Youth for Christ to help young people to share their faith. It's about realising the value of your own story, God's story and the stories of other people. The course enables young people to adopt great listening skills, go deeper into knowing more of God's story, to see the value of their own and others' stories, and change their relationships for ever. For further information visit www.theartofconnecting.org.

General

- **yfcONE HOPE Teams.** Youth for Christ have been offering opportunities for young people to engage in mission for over 25 years; using the diverse God given skills and abilities young people bring to impact the lives of other young people where it matters most. yfcONE during HOPE 08 are looking for volunteers and locations to enable effective mission to take place; working in prisons, on the streets, in schools, using sport, drama, dance and great youth work to connect with young people. An additional team will be recruited as part of the specialist HOPE teams working in villages, towns and cities near you to make an impact. If you are eighteen to twenty-five and up for the challenge, contact us on www.yfcone.com. Youth for Christ also offer a full mission consultation and delivery package for your area, helping you to deliver mission in a language young people understand.

- **Teenagers in Scotland** can get involved with Fire Starters – a group of Christians who meet together once a month to share God's life and love with one another and with the nation. Fire Starters also provide ongoing leadership training and equipping.
Find out more at www.firestartersuk.org and www.myspace/firestartersforjesus.

- **For young people interested in sport,** Christians in Sport have Bible studies, talks and CDs specifically tailored for them that you can buy or download for free at www.christiansinsport.org.uk/youth_sport/youth_resources.htm.

- **Different denominations employ Youth Officers** – try getting in touch with your local representative and consider who else is working with youth in your area to see if you can work together.

- **Be inspired by 24-7 prayer,** a missionary movement started by young people that has been founded on prayer. Find out more at www.24-7prayer.com.

Publications

- **Xcelerate:** *The evangelist's heartbeat*, Matt Wilson and Andy Hawthorne. This book contains valuable lessons from The Message Evangelism Training School in Manchester connected with the Eden and Tribe projects. £6.99 from www.standrewsbookshop.co.uk.

- **12 Disciples,** Andy Flannagan with Anne Calver. Featuring gritty, unforgettable stories of faith, hope and love that highlight how young people connected to Youth for Christ are being good news. Their stories are aligned with teaching on the story of another disciple who experienced similar ups and downs on his journey – Simon Peter. £7.99 from www.lion-publishing.co.uk.

- **Mission-shaped Youth,** Tim Sudworth, Graham Cray, Chris Russell. Following on from *Mission-shaped Church*, this book examines what

End notes:
1: See Judith Harris, *The Nurture Assumption* (Touchstone Press, 1999). Available from www.amazon.co.uk.
2: *The 2005 English Church Census* (London: Christian Research Association).
3: The 2001 National Census (England and Wales), The 2001 Scottish Census and The 2001 Northern Ireland Census

it means to have a 'youth-mission-shaped church' and challenges us to intersect with today's young people in their daily lives and culture. The authors urge us to offer a mission that isn't just about evangelism, but is also about supporting pastorally and spiritually. £7.99 from www.chpublishing.co.uk.

- **Young People and Mission,** edited by David Brooker. This book grapples with subjects that include helping teenagers to share their faith, ecology and mission, living in a multi-faith society and making the most of a gap year. Challenging, practical, informative and insightful, *Young People and Mission* will help us to re-think the way we do mission with and to young people – inside and outside the church. £8.99 from www.chpublishing.co.uk.

- **The Manga Bible.** The Bible is brought to life in a new way using the dynamic style of Manga comics (the fastest growing genre in British and American publishing). Particularly suitable for teenagers and young adults *The Manga Bible* is a faithful interpretation of the scriptures using beautiful and dramatic artwork. See more details at www.themangabible.co.uk. £8.99 from www.hodderchristianbooks.co.uk.

- **Live the Life,** Mike Pilavachi and Craig Borlase. This funny and accessible book encourages teenagers to follow Jesus in all areas of their life. £7.99 from www.hodderchristianbooks.co.uk.

- **SUbmerge** is designed to encourage eleven to fourteen-year-olds develop a habit of reading their Bible helping them to engage through music, reflection, art and communicating with others. Published every two months (from October 2007) for £2 per copy (subscriptions available). See www.scriptureunion.org.uk for more detail and to order. For resources from Scripture Union Scotland see www.suscotland.org.uk, for Scripture Union Northern Ireland see www.suni.co.uk

CHANGE ME
AND WE CAN CHANGE OUR WORLD.

"I have seen the work of Compassion first hand and know that it makes an incredible difference to some of the most needy children of the world."

ANDY HAWTHORNE
Director of the Message Trust

By changing the lives of individual children, your church can help to change the world. Compassion seeks out some of the world's most vulnerable children and with the help of churches like yours, provides them with the skills and opportunities they need to change their lives and the lives of those around them. Working exclusively through local churches in developing countries, Compassion ensures that there is financial integrity, long term commitment and the opportunity for every child to hear and respond to the good news of Jesus Christ.

TO FIND OUT HOW YOUR CHURCH CAN SPONSOR CHILDREN AND MAKE A POSITIVE IMPACT IN IMPOVERISHED COMMUNITIES VISIT WWW.COMPASSIONUK.ORG OR CALL 01932 836490

Releasing children from poverty
Compassion®
in Jesus' name

Compassion UK   43 High Street   Weybridge   Surrey KT13 8BB   Registered Charity Number 1077216

'HOPE 08 is bringing people and churches together, serving God and the local community. It is amazing to see so many people from across the country involved.'

'Partnership is really at the heart and I want to invite and encourage every person who knows and owns the name of Jesus Christ to become a partner of HOPE.'

CHAPTER 10

HOPE IN SCHOOLS AND COLLEGES

**Ian Henderson (The Message),
Rich Wilson (Fusion),
Jamie Haith (Student Alpha –
colleges and universities)**

It would be difficult to find a more exciting opportunity for a church wanting to connect with and serve the children, young people and their families in their community.

HOPE IN SCHOOLS

Schools are often the hub of the community; 99 per cent of young people spend most of their time there (or at least should do!). It would be difficult to find a more exciting opportunity for a church wanting to connect with and serve the children, young people and their families in their community, yet surprisingly many churches don't get involved with their local school. Often this is because we feel that we haven't been invited to, we don't think we have anything to offer or because we're focused on other ministries. We believe 2008 is a great time to change this, to get stuck into supporting local schools and reaching hundreds of young people.

basis: helping with the washing up, listening to children read, serving on the board of governors or Parent and Teachers Association and raising funds for the school. Also, don't underestimate the impact you can have just by doing what you say you will – reliability is highly prized among staff who have seen many people make promises and then not deliver on them.

GREAT IDEAS

- **Ask the school what they need:** It's a simple place to start, but once you know the needs of the school, you'll know where you can serve.
- **Assemblies:** If you've got the gift of the gab this may be for you. If you don't but you have a car you could give someone a lift – there's nothing worse than being late for an assembly because you can't find a parking space.
- **Crafts: Are you artistic?** Then offer your skills. A lot of primary school teachers may want to use art and craft activities in class but may not have the time/gifts to prepare stuff in advance.
- **Christian Union:** Does your secondary school have one? Could you support the young people in your church to start one? Could you help them book speakers, do publicity etc.?
- **Discovery course:** Alpha and others provide materials to run a course to help young people think, question and discover the Christian faith. Many schools would be happy for a course to take place at lunchtime or after school, particularly if pupils were requesting it. See Chapter 7 for more details on courses.
- **Dance:** Streetdance, breakdance, ballet, even line dancing can make for a great after-school club.
- **Employ a schools worker:** Could your church or a group of churches employ a full- or part-time schools worker?
- **Fundraisers:** Most schools need books, computers and other equipment. What crazy schemes can you come up with or how can you work with what the school is planning to raise money?

Beware!
1. What are our motives?
There are some incredible opportunities to serve our local schools, but the key words are 'to serve'. It's important to stop and check our motives for working in schools; do we just want to promote our church youth club/event? Are we there because we just want more bums on pews? Or are we there because we care about the education of the children and want to support the school? Young people can see through a sales pitch and will know if you're insincere. Teachers will not be impressed if you are insensitive to school rules and do altar calls in assemblies. These kinds of mistakes can damage relationships between schools and all the churches in the area so respect the fact that you are a guest at the school and are there to help.

2. What research have we done?
Before you start making any plans, find out what is already going on. Are there other churches/ organisations working in the school? Are any of the teachers Christians? Pick up the phone and start asking around. There are some fantastic resources available to help you deliver effective schools work (Many are available or linked to www.hope08.com.) Spend time looking and reading as much as you can. If you are new to schools work, maybe you could ask to 'shadow' a local schools worker.

3. What can we offer?
It's easy to fall into the trap of thinking that only people with big mouths and baggy jeans can do something in a school. Yet all over the country Christians are involved in schools on a voluntary

There are some incredible opportunities to serve our local schools, but the key words are 'to serve'.

- **Guest weeks:** Many schools are willing to have guests as part of the school's programme. Christian theatre, dance and music all work extremely well. Visit www.hope08.com for more information about organisations that are available to be booked by churches to work in schools.

- **The HOPE Revolution:** encourage your young people to join the HOPE revolution at www.hope-revolution.com which will give them loads of ideas for impacting their school.

- **Lunch clubs:** Ask the school if you can start a 45 minute–one hour club with games, activities and talks or get involved with one that is already running.

- **Music:** Are you a DJ or musician? You could teach your skills or run hands-on workshops during lunchtimes or after school.

- **Pray for schools:** Prayer is a key way to serve your local school. Get a group of people who are prepared to meet for an hour once a week to pray for each of the schools. Write to the head teachers to let them know the church is praying, to ask if there are key times they would appreciate prayers (e.g. during exams) and if they have any prayer requests. For primary schools, offer to read out in services/put on the walls any prayers that pupils send to the church. The Schools Prayer Network exists to stimulate and encourage committed Christian prayer for every school in the UK – visit www.schoolsprayernetwork.org.uk or www.suscotland.org.uk for more information.

HOPE CHALLENGE: This is a national social action initiative which enables churches and schools to work together to make a difference by bringing hope to their community. Schools compete against each other to raise money for a chosen charity and to bring physical change to their area through social action projects. For more information visit www.hope08.com

- **Parent and Teacher Association:** Are you a parent? This is a great way to get involved and to get to know some of the other parents and teachers.

- **Reading:** Could you sit with primary school pupils as they read to you?

- **Support Christian teachers:** Meet with them regularly to pray and encourage them in their work, and to share ideas for how the church can continue to serve the school.

- **Sports clubs:** Before or after school you could help with coaching a sports club.

- **School productions:** Many schools have a school play and would love help with costumes and scenery etc.

Of course, this isn't a complete list, but hopefully it's beginning to help you to see some of the many ways you could serve your local schools.

HOPE IN COLLEGES AND UNIVERSITIES

There are now more than 2.25million students in the UK, which means that each autumn 40 per cent of young people now migrate to form small cities within cities. The student group is fast becoming the largest clearly defined unreached group in the UK with only around one per cent being Christian. Annually, around eight to twelve thousand churches unwittingly send Christian men and women to live among this people group for three to four years. The vast majority have received no training, no equipping, and no envisioning for what to expect or of the difference they could make.

The last ten years has seen the average age of conversion rise to twenty-one and students are arguably at their most experimental, teachable, and more open to influence than at any other time in their life.

A number of churches help to prepare their students for university life through pre-university training days and weekends. For many years students have been linked up with university Christian Unions through the UCCF link up scheme – visit www.uccf.org.uk/newstudents to find out more and get connected.

Understanding the universities

There is most certainly an institutional nervousness towards the promotion of and invitation to the Christian faith. Universities are now huge service providers, incubators of new businesses, multimillion-pound international enterprises and research hubs.

It seems students are encouraged to think freely but not so freely as to evoke too much passion or activism, whether it be religious, political or otherwise. This has implications for the proclamation of the gospel and seeing students make Jesus their Lord. The university institution delegates oversight to chaplains for all faith-based activity on campuses or university property.

The chaplaincy seeks to act as the umbrella for all religious groups in universities. If you intend to do a mission on a campus it is sensible to try and gain the support of the chaplaincy. Missions and related activity have to be run by the students themselves and external parties must be invited in by the students. In many institutions this has been done very effectively through the student led Christian Unions.

Churches are essential to the future of student mission. They provide stability and continuity of vision in the midst of a very transient culture – they are both a refuge and sending base for students. We hope the ideas below will serve to encourage and build confidence in church leaders, student workers and cell leaders to do more for students during HOPE 08 and beyond.

GREAT IDEAS

- **Ask the university what they need,** introduce your church and any services you can offer. It may be that you approach the institution, student union and chaplaincy separately, as they may not be well connected. Also ask the students involved in the Christian Union how you can better support them and find out what organisations are already involved with mission on the campus.

The student group is fast becoming the largest clearly defined unreached group in the UK with only around one per cent being Christian.

- **Campaigns:** Working with student groups and student unions on global issues that show Christians care and are prepared to turn words into action. Many excellent resources can be found at the Speak and Tearfund sites www.speak.org.uk/campaigns and www.tearfund.org/youth/students.
- **Cell groups (small groups):** We believe cells are the most effective, grassroots way of being good news to fellow students. Ask one of your students to start a cell as the foundation for ongoing mission. Free cell notes are available from www.fusion.uk.com.
- **Chaplaincy:** Talk to chaplains, get to know them, find out what they do and where the local church can serve.
- **Discovery courses:** Many students readily attend courses such as Alpha, Christianity Explored or Essence. These can be run on or off campus in cafés, homes or church buildings. (See Chapter 7.)

- **Employ a student worker:** Could your church or a group of churches employ a full or part-time student worker? Fusion provides training and ongoing support throughout the year. See www.fusion.uk.com/ studentworkers.
- **Fresher fairs:** Some universities have over three hundred stalls, half of which are paid for by external organisations. While competing for profile in these places is a huge turn off to the majority of churches – can churches afford not to be there? Beyond these challenges lie opportunities for mission, breaking down negative Christian stereotypes, working together and a chance to think imaginatively about your stall and bring hope.

- **Fairtrade:** At present only 40 of 120 universities are Fairtrade but there are lots of resources for students and churches to change this. Consider starting or joining a campaign and launching it with a Fairtrade fashion show. See www.fairtrade.org.uk/get_involved_university.htm.

- **Free drinks:** An easy way to bless the student population is to hand out water and other drinks after club nights to thirsty, drunk and dehydrated students. Some Student Unions supply these at cost or even free.

- **Link-up:** Prepare your students for getting involved in HOPE 08 before they go to university and link them to a church in their place of study through the Fusion link-up, personal contact, church links, and the various organisations working with students including UCCF, Christians in Sport, Navigators, Agape, CMF and Friends International. See useful websites for details.

- **Loveyouruni:** The universities need to know that Christians love them and we have some stereotypes to change. Churches and their students can find a whole load of ways to demonstrate the reality of God's love through acts of kindness. More ideas on www.loveyouruni.org.

- **Off campus:** This is where most students live and it may be much easier to serve, connect with and advertise to them. Identify the main student areas and what is needed.

- **Pray for universities:** Prayer is a vital way to serve your local college or university. Gather a group of people who are prepared to meet for an hour once a week to pray for local universities. Write to the vice chancellor to let them know the church is praying, to ask if there are key times they would appreciate prayers and if they have any prayer requests. Use the prayer guide to pray through the academic year for students. Downloads are available from various groups – see useful websites.

- **Reconcile:** Work with the university, student union and local authority to bridge some of

Student Alpha Many youth and student organisations are on board with the Alpha Challenge to make sure every university Fresher is invited to a Student Alpha course in 2008. Find out more www.studentalpha.org/students.

Churches are essential to the future of student mission.

the 'town and gown' divide. Offer to take a community warden post that involves chatting to noisy students and being a mediator.

- **Student unions:** Many Christian groups are working closely with student unions and have developed a strong connection. Talk to your student union about possible areas of collaboration.

- **Support Christian lecturers:** Meet with them regularly to pray and encourage them in their work and to share ideas for how the church can serve them.

- **Societies:** Can be started with anything from twelve to twenty-five students signing up, depending on the university. Across the universities there is an increasing diversity of Christian and other religious groups and more societies are starting up.

Check back to the websites regularly as this list will get longer as 2008 approaches!

Universities and Colleges Christian Fellowship (UCCF): UCCF is made up of 350 Christian Unions committed to proclaiming the gospel to students in a way that is relevant, engaging and persuasive. As part of HOPE 08 these unions will undertake over ninety mission weeks aiming to give every resident student a copy of Mark's Gospel. This mass 450,000 Gospel distribution will be used to invite students to lunchtime dialogues and discussion groups, meals with a message, films with a short talk and other such events. Find out more about UCCF at www.uccf.org.uk.
Pod Bhogal, UCCF Communications Director

Student groups – there are a number of different models of student outreach that you might find helpful including Uccf:thechristianunions ('living and speaking for Jesus'), Christians in Sport, Navigators and Agape.
The best models flow out of working with local churches - see useful websites for more details.

Schools work – XLP Gunz Down Tour

A Mori survey for the Youth Justice Board found that *29 per cent of eleven - to sixteen-year-old school pupils admitted to carrying a knife*. Some schools now have security measures and personnel to relieve students of potentially lethal weaponry as they enter school, but this merely treats a symptom. New weapons are easily found to replace those confiscated and taking them away doesn't address the reasons why young people are carrying knives in the first place.

At XLP (a charity working in schools in south-east London), we decided to tackle the problem head on and to encourage eleven- to fourteen-year-olds to make courageous life choices concerning crime and violence; choices that would enable them to avoid becoming eighteen-year-old prisoners.

'We decided the best way to communicate with this age group was through music, drama, film and by giving them positive role models they could relate to and aspire to be like,' says Patrick Regan, Director of XLP. 'We worked with hip hop band GreenJade to come up with a show that aims to achieve real transformation of hearts and minds concerning issues of violence, crime and weapons.'

Both hard-hitting and entertaining, GreenJade's hour-long performance combines music, drama, competitions and film, and uses the school's main halls for a lesson period. The show is then followed up by a series of lessons on respect and responsibility, which can be incorporated into the RE and PSHE syllabus.

The hope is that by exposing the dark reality of making bad choices, we can inform the youth and young people that there are good life choices and that it's worth being courageous. We intend to empower young people to choose and give them access to materials that will help them to assess their potential actions.

The show demonstrates that wrong choices lead to more wrong choices which eventually lead to you being defined by those choices. Right choices allow you a freedom to choose your path through life, to explore opportunities and relationships, to aspire to be like your heroes. Your choices are crucial to understanding who you are. Our aim is to 'cultivate another choice'.

To date, Gunz Down has been run in 30 schools in London, five in Manchester, ten in Birmingham and ten in Nottingham. If guns and knives are a problem for young people in your area see www.gunzdown.com to find out how you can run a tour in your schools.

RESOURCES

The HOPE 08 website will provide links to many resources available to buy or download including a students, churches and chaplaincies paper, lesson and assembly materials and lunch club ideas – see www.hope08.com.

- **Support Your Local School:** A guide to opportunities for church involvement in schools. A downloadable PDF file with the nuts and bolts of how you can work in your local schools.
- **Effective Schoolswork:** A book written by experienced schools worker, Lee Jackson. Available as a free download. www.schoolsministrynetwork.co.uk. Includes tips on how to approach schools.
- **You can download resources** for Christian clubs in secondary schools from the Re:source section of the Scripture Union website www.scriptureunion.org.uk. For resources from Scripture Union Scotland see www.suscotland.org.uk, for Scripture Union Northern Ireland see www.suni.co.uk.
- **Sport is a popular and accessible subject** for young people and can be easily linked to Christian values. Get free downloads for youth leaders and teachers, from practical 'how to' fact sheets through to assembly outlines, from www.christiansinsport.org.uk.

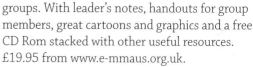

- **'Book of Hope'** produce a number of editions aimed at school-age children (five to eight, eight to eleven, eleven to fourteen and fifteen to twenty), helping children looking at issues like self-esteem, caring for others, peaceful problem solving and understanding their purpose in life. Younger additions include games and exercises while older versions have a magazine style. There are also accompanying Teacher's Manuals. Find out more and order at www.bookofhope.co.uk.
- **The Youth Emmaus** course is designed to help those aged eleven to sixteen explore the basics of the Christian faith and can be run in schools during lunchtime or as after school study

> Helping children looking at issues like self-esteem, caring for others, peaceful problem solving and understanding their purpose in life.

groups. With leader's notes, handouts for group members, great cartoons and graphics and a free CD Rom stacked with other useful resources. £19.95 from www.e-mmaus.org.uk.
- *Jam* **magazine** contains interviews, articles about films and issues facing teenagers. Order at www.jammag.co.uk for £1.99.
- **Scripture Union** produces a number of resources suitable for use in schools and with school-age children:

  - They hold two five-day residential training courses 'Training in Schools Work' and 'Advanced School for Schools Workers'.
  - *So, Why God?*, *Streetwise*, *Awesome*, *Rocky Road* and *Bulls Eye* are materials that can be used with school-age children looking to find out more about God, answering questions on why there is suffering, why we pray and who God and Jesus are. £9.99.
  - *Into the Bible – 101 routes to explore* is aimed at Keystage 2 children and includes material to equip teachers of all faith backgrounds to use the material with integrity (this could be a good resource for your church to buy your local school).
  - 'Top Tips' is a series of booklets which includes the titles *Reaching unchurched children*, *Growing families with faith* and *Welcoming children of other faiths*. £2.99 each or four for £10.

Find out more about these and other training and resources at www.scriptureunion.org.uk (click on Training or Resources). For resources from Scripture Union Scotland see www.suscotland.org.uk, for Scripture Union Northern Ireland see www.suni.co.uk.
- **Assemblies Resource Book** and *Assemblies Resources Through the Year* are full of ideas for fresh and fun assemblies in primary schools covering stories from the Bible and Festivals of World Religions. £10.99 from www.spck.org.uk. You can also access ideas online at www.assemblies.org.uk.

The Big Deal is an initiative that is planning to host a High Schools Mission in the vast majority of Greater Manchester's high schools. Find out more at www.bigdeal.org.uk.

Other useful websites

www.agape.org.uk/students

www.christiansinsport.org.uk

www.cmf.org.uk

www.fairtrade.org.uk/get_involved_university.htm

www.ficu.edu

www.fusion.uk.com

www.loveyouruni.org

www.navigators.co.uk

www.peopleandplanet.org/ftunis

www.relessonsonline.com

www.schoolswork.co.uk

www.speak.org.uk/campaigns

www.alpha.org/students

www.talkingdonkey.co.uk

www.tearfund.org/youth/students

www.uccf.org.uk

'From its beginning HOPE 08 has been an ecumenical initiative which can thus witness to the power of the gospel to unite people in a world of many divisions.'

'HOPE 08 is a God-given opportunity for the church to work together and share the good news of Jesus in all its fullness.'

CHAPTER 11

HOPE OVER THE SUMMER

**Phil Hulks (Re:Act – Urban Saints),
Richard Shaw (Scripture Union),
Marty Woods (Fusion),
Dee Buchanan (Youth for Christ)**

With the extended holidays, longer evenings and warmer days, the summer is a great time to bless our communities and to get young people actively involved in putting on events and running missions.

There are two main ways you could get your church involved in HOPE over the summer:

1. They could come up with an idea for an event and then make it happen.

2. You could get a team such as those from Re:Act to come and support your young people in setting up an event.

GREAT IDEAS

1. DIY – Running an event yourself

Putting on a free event for your community is a great way to build relationships, bless people and, ultimately, to show God's love. It doesn't matter how many of you there are or how small or large your budget, you can come up with something that will get people talking.

- **Try and have a minimum of three partner churches.** This will help to demonstrate to the local community the Christian church is working together for them. Representatives from these churches will also form the organising group for the event.

- **Each project should look to develop a partnership** with the local council, community groups and police (see Chapter 16 for more details). These are key relationships to establish, creating gateways into community funding and resources; they will also help in identifying projects such as social action and youth outreach activities.

- **Projects will need to undertake risk assessments,** which means carrying out checks for things such as health and safety, considering what might go wrong and how risks can be reduced. Few activities are risk free, but preparation and planning can reduce the risk for most activities. Many of the HOPE 08 partners are able to advise in the preparation of risk assessments – contact the HOPE office on 01273 571939 or info@hope08.com. Risk assessments are required for insurance (a partner church can extend its existing policy to cover the projects) and health and safety.

- **Projects will need to establish a Child Protection Policy** and should consider adapting one from one of the partner churches involved in the project. The project will also need to consider if a Criminal Records Bureau check has been carried out for those working with children or vulnerable people.

How it could work:

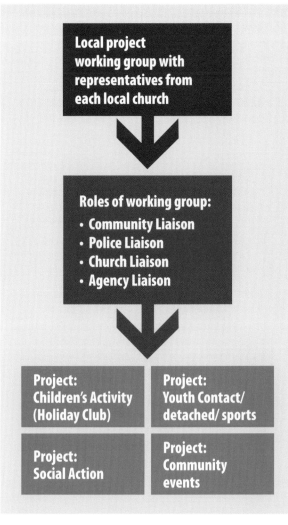

Local project working group with representatives from each local church

↓

Roles of working group:
- Community Liaison
- Police Liaison
- Church Liaison
- Agency Liaison

↓

Project: Children's Activity (Holiday Club)

Project: Youth Contact/ detached/ sports

Project: Social Action

Project: Community events

There are hundreds of project examples. Here are just a few to get you thinking about the possibilities for the summer of 2008. A lot of these activities could be run alone or with one of the teams covered in the next section.

- **Community barbecues**, fun days or evenings with bouncy castles and kids games.
- **Children's Holiday Club.**
- **Café drop-ins** for young mums and older folk.
- **Youth drop-ins,** detached work and play and sport leadership.

Putting on a free event for your community is a great way to build relationships, bless people and, ultimately, to show God's love.

Friendly atmosphere, great activities, high levels of fun, all free of charge.

- **Evangelistic concerts.**
- **Rubbish and litter** clear-ups in parks, council communal areas and along the street.
- **Cutting back of communal gardens,** parks and other areas where plants have overgrown.
- **General landscaping** to enhance a local area.
- **Street drama,** storyboards, worship on the streets.
- **Older people's ministry** including cream tea parties, afternoon tea dances, sing-alongs.

2. Events supported by teams from Christian youth organisations

A number of organisations will make teams available to support your church. Some will require payment, others are self-funded.

- **Re:Act** (originally Urban Saints/DNA): As part of HOPE 08, multiple teams of young people, evangelists and bands are being trained and made available to villages, towns and cities all over the UK, to work alongside local churches in putting on two great events in the summer of 2008.

1. Family Fun Day: Friendly atmosphere, great activities, high levels of fun, all of which (including a barbecue and outdoor café) are free of charge to your community. This is a truly fantastic opportunity for churches in your locality to join together in demonstrating God's amazing unconditional love, acceptance and generosity towards people in your community. Following the family fun day, guests are invited to stay on to Church Outdoors. A short gap between the two events, plus clear communication as to what is happening next, allows guests to opt in or opt out.

2. Church Outdoors: Taking the church service outdoors and presenting the good news of Jesus in a high quality and fun way, relevant and sensitive to seekers; challenging, yet life-changing to those who respond. A pre-planned local follow-up strategy will be implemented to assist new Christians and seekers in their personal faith journey.

To make these events happen Re:Act will provide:

- A comprehensive information pack including a step-by-step guide on how to host a Re:Act day in your locality;

- Access to a DVD training resource on friendship evangelism, written and delivered by Pete Gilbert from DNA, specifically designed to help the church congregations prepare for the day and maximise the effectiveness of the Re:Act mission;

- A team of approximately sixty people including a live band, evangelist, road show team and young people who have just completed a three-day residential training course;

- Equipment: Mobile stage (articulated lorry plus additional staging), generator, PA, four inflatable attractions, two gazebos, four large barbecues, seven sets of patio tables and chairs, hair-braiding, face-painting and balloon-modelling materials;

- Promotional materials: Five thousand family fun day flyers.

If your church or group of churches would like to use a Re:Act team, you will need to provide:

- A fee of £2,100;

- Food and accommodation for the Re:Act team for one night;

Taking the church service outdoors and presenting the good news of Jesus in a high quality and fun way.

- Food and drinks for the family fun day barbecue;

- Additional family fun day activities and people to help out on the day;

- A minimum of five young people aged fourteen plus to join the Re:Act team.

More information about Re:Act 2008 and application forms are available on www.hope08.com and www.urbansaints.org/react or call Bernie Wheeler on 01582 589836.

- **Fire Starters:** Fire Starters are an organisation in Scotland that can make teams available to serve local churches in youth and children's outreach activities. They also provide training for young leaders. Find out more at www.firestartersuk.org.

- **Youth for Christ teams:** YFC are also looking to make teams of between four and ten young people available to serve churches for ten days over the summer. When your church has come up with its summer plans, contact Dee Buchanan at Youth for Christ to see if one of the YFC teams can come and join you: dee.buchanan@yfc.co.uk or call 0121 550 8055.

- **On the Move:** On the Move is a Christian organisation that works with churches across a town or city to set up free community barbecues. They provide a visible and friendly environment with sung worship, outdoor seating and local church members inviting those on the streets to come and join in free. Find out about how On the Move can help you set up a mission barbecue in your town by visiting www.onthemove.org.uk.

Other great ideas for the summer

- **'Open crowd' festivals:** Summer is a great time to hold an 'open crowd' festival, an idea developed by Fusion Youth and Community UK. The events bring the local community together in all its diversity; multicultural, multi-generational and multi-denominational. At its heart it has the local Christians working

fresh expressions
changing church for a changing world

A fresh expression of church is a new or different form of church for our changing culture established primarily for the benefit of those who are not yet members of any church.

A sign of hope in our generation are the new congregations which begin as Christians love and serve and listen to their neighbours.

Available now:

'expressions' the dvd 1 and 2

Three booklets ideal for small groups:
- Moving on in a Mission Shaped Church
- Starting a Fresh Expression
- Listening for Mission

All available from your local Christian bookshop or www.chpublishing.co.uk

vision days
❖ dream your dreams and share your story
❖ ask your questions and think about what it means to be church
❖ discover the resources available and build relationships

mission shaped intro
❖ a six week course aiming to change the way we think
❖ fun and interactive
❖ putting mission to the top of the agenda
❖ ideal for all Christians

mission shaped ministry
❖ a one year, part-time course equipping you for new forms of ministry
❖ designed for individuals and teams starting or involved in fresh expressions
❖ teaching by local and national teachers

Contact us through the website to enquire about training in your area or to view our resources

Fresh Expressions is an initiative of the Archbishops of Canterbury and York supported by the Methodist Council and working in partnership with a range of other bodies and churches.

Fresh Expressions Ltd, 15 Fyfield Road, Oxford, OX2 6QE

www.freshexpressions.org.uk

Company no. 3598030 Registered Charity no. 1080103

together to love and serve the local community in such a way that they can experience something of the kingdom in a safe and inclusive atmosphere. The idea is to run such a festival as part of a three-year integrated strategy for reaching your community. Fusion Youth and Community UK can help you develop it alongside Christmas festivals and pageants, Easter outreaches, St George's Day outreach events, and also provide a hundred other highly focused outreach opportunities that you can choose from that are being used around the world.

Fusion Youth and Community can offer training and support to assist you to develop a strategic three- to five-year plan for the transformation of your community. Start with an 'Open crowd' festival and see how you can contact hundreds of people in your local area, giving them an experience where they will be hungry for more. Want to know more? Contact the Fusion Youth and Community UK office by email on office@fusionyac.org.

- **Summer festivals:** A number of Christian organisations are committed to making their summer festivals as welcoming as possible for those interested in the Christian faith. There will also be special teaching programmes at events aimed at equipping and inspiring people to get involved with word and deed mission. See our website for more details of all events and festivals focusing on HOPE 08, www.hope08.com.
- **Christian Vocations** produce a Short Term Service Directory each year with details of almost a hundred programmes both here and abroad and also have a Mission Matters pack containing articles, information and current vacancies with sixty Christian agencies. For more information and to order visit www.christianvocations.org.

It's going to be a sports mad summer!

Euro 2008 and Olympics

It's going to be a sports mad summer with Euro 2008 kicking off in Austria and Switzerland in June and the Olympics in Beijing starting on 8 August. This gives us loads of great opportunities to host community activities around these events, particularly for young people. Why not

- Put all the games up on a big screen in church;
- Hold a mini-community Olympics;
- Run PlayStation nights and have FIFA football computer competitions with football-themed prizes;
- Hold a 24 hour sport event to raise money for charity;
- Take a group to a local sporting event;
- Hold a night themed around the different countries competing in Euro 2008 and the Olympics with traditional foods and activities to help people learn about the country's customs;
- Put on a week or weekend-long sports camp with tournaments, competitions, time to watch matches and to do talks that link sport with God and moral values.

• **The Big Deal:** Big Deal weekends will be happening all over Manchester involving community action, large-scale family fun days and youth concerts, encouraging the church in Manchester to play its part in HOPE 08, delivering one million hours of kindness (see Chapter 6). The Big Deal has an extraordinary record of partnership with local churches, the police and local authorities and has developed a range of resources and ideas to equip local churches across the county to deliver their own community action initiatives. These can all be found at www.bigdeal.org.uk.

Hope-filled Prayer

Over fifty thousand young people attend Christian events and holidays through the summer, with the potential of more to be involved during HOPE 08. Why not encourage the adults in your church to be praying for a young person during the summer? Visit www.prayforthesummer.co.uk for dates and prayer points.

If you get a lot of visitors to your church then why not hold a prayer open day?

This great press article (right) which shows positive community response was received after a Re:Act event. For more information about working with the media see Chapter 16.

CASE STUDY

Wiltshire Times
Family fun day proves big success

HUNDREDS of families descended on Trowbridge Park on Wednesday for a free family fun day.

Trowbridge churches joined together to help put on the event, including Trowbridge Christian youth group, Impax.

'We wanted to give the community something free without the stress of having to pay.'

There was a road show with a live band, face painting, hair braiding, balloon modelling and a barbecue with teas and coffees all for free.

Younger children could enjoy a play area and there were inflatables for children to play on too.

Becky Cousins' children, Ruth, 11 and William, eight, who go to West Ashton Primary School enjoyed going to the Talk Talk Tent where children could talk to someone to learn more about God.

Mrs Cousins said: 'It's just nice to have a picnic in the park with your friends.

'It's very unusual for things like this to be free. We've got four mums and 15 children here and it's been great.'

Christine Fox, whose children, Lauren, 10 and Annabelle, eight, enjoyed having their faces painted, agreed.

She said: 'It's nice to have an event to go to that doesn't have to cost a fortune.'

Captain Heather Godwin, of the Salvation Army, who was co-ordinating the day, said: 'It has been brilliant it couldn't be better.

'We wanted to give the community something free without the stress of having to pay.'

The day was rounded off with a concert including a puppet show, worship, dancing, interviews, games and competitions. (See http://www.wiltshiretimes.co.uk/search/display. var.865215.0.family_fun_day_proves_big_success.php)

RESOURCES

• Want to put on a sporting event?

Download great fact sheets and 'how to' guides from the Christians in Sport website, including how to run a sports tournament, how to put on a big screen event and how to run a sports holiday club. Visit www.christiansinsport.org.uk

• **MJK** is a ministry that uses a state-of-the-art concert-truck with inbuilt stage, PA and lighting. It uses rappers, DJs and evangelists to get the gospel message across. Open to working alongside churches in a variety of outreach settings, some of which might include fun days, street outreaches and youth events. Find out more by contacting MJK at www.makejesusknown.com, emailing info@makejesusknown.com or calling 0161 728 1522.

• **Champions Challenge** is a holiday club based on Mark's Gospel with games, drama and craft all around an Olympics theme. Order your pack (available from December 2007) for £9.99 from www.scriptureunion.org.uk. For resources from Scripture Union Scotland see www.suscotland.org.uk, for Scripture Union Northern Ireland see www.suni.co.uk.

• **KidzKlubs** are an excellent way to reach out to communities either as a one-off holiday club or as part of an on-going programme. There are currently hundreds of KidzKlubs operating across the UK and beyond. For more information on how to run a KidzKlub and resources please visit www.kidzklub.biz.

CHAPTER 12

HOPE-FILLED PRAYER

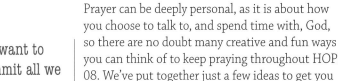

Jane Holloway
(World Prayer Centre),
Liza Hoeksma (Soul Survivor)

Prayer is right at the heart of HOPE 08; so much so that we dedicated 2007 to be a Year of Prayer in preparation for all that we would do. Because so many elements of HOPE 08 are about practical activities, it would be easy to come up with some great ideas, get focused on being busy and realise we somehow left God a little bit out of the process. Instead we want to commit all we do to God, to make sure we depend on his strength and not our own and allow him to challenge and speak to us at every step along the way. As we connect with him about the issues surrounding us in our communities, as we cry out to him for the people we are getting to know, as we seek him both personally and corporately, we will find ourselves in a position where he can change our hearts to be more like his.

> We want to commit all we do to God, to make sure we depend on his strength.

GREAT IDEAS

Prayer can be deeply personal, as it is about how you choose to talk to, and spend time with, God, so there are no doubt many creative and fun ways you can think of to keep praying throughout HOPE 08. We've put together just a few ideas to get you started and to help you find things that work for you and your church.

- **Start the year with a HOPE-filled prayer:** We'd love 2008 to start with Christians uniting together all across the UK to make the same request to God – that we would see our nation significantly changed in 2008. This could be what some people call their *Watch Night Service* as you gather your church together to see out the old year with worship, prayer and celebration; a great opportunity to focus on praying for hope to be released in our communities and for many to come to faith. Or you could find time within your usual plans of going to a party or having dinner with friends to say the five-minute prayer that you can download from our website – www.hope08.com.

- **Prayer and fasting:** Many churches begin the year with a period of prayer and fasting to dedicate the coming 12 months to God. It would be a fantastic way to start 2008 by praying and fasting for the change we long to see as we all bring HOPE 08 to our villages, towns and cities. Of course it's up to you how long you fast for and what you give up – it could be food or something else that has an important place in your life such as TV, coffee or alcohol.

• **Prayer for unity:** With unity among churches being one of the key themes of HOPE 08 you could get on board with the Week of Prayer for Christian Unity which happens 18–25 January. See www.ctbi.org.uk – Churches Together in Britain and Ireland for the 2008 theme and to download prayers.

• **Prayer triplets:** Prayer triplets have been a popular way to commit to regularly praying for friends who aren't Christians. They involve three Christians praying both on their own and together for three friends with whom they are in regular contact. With the emphasis on evangelism in 2008, we'd love to encourage as many people as possible to form prayer triplets – perhaps that go right through the year or, say, from Easter to HOPE Explored in September. Most prayer triplets meet weekly and yours could be linked to your cell or small group in the church or workplace, rather than as an additional meeting. Either way, find the best time and place that works for your triplet – you'll be more likely to stick to it. You can download prayer triplet cards from www.hope08.com.

• **A creative prayer night:** Everyone likes to express their prayers in different ways so why not hold an evening at your church that incorporates a variety of ways to pray? People are free to move to whichever activity or station

Many churches begin the year with a period of prayer and fasting to dedicate the coming 12 months to God.

that suits them and then move on as they like. For example

- Have space and provide resources for people who would like to draw or paint as a way to express their prayers to God;

- Bring the local and national newspapers so people can go through them and pray for the people and issues reported;

- Provide a place for quiet contemplation for those who would like to sit in silence and meditate on a cross or passages from the Bible;

- Offer a corner with pens and paper where people can write down their prayer requests (they can either take them away if they are personal or leave them pinned to a cross);

- Put up paper on a wall and ask people to write the names of those in the community who need prayer. They can write the prayer requests or leave it simply as a name, others come and pray for those people, then add their own names.

• **Use a prayer labyrinth:** Prayer labyrinths are a tradition that date back to the twelfth century but have been brought up to date by being available online at sites like www.rejesus. co.uk/spirituality/labyrinth. Labyrinths have three stages: an inward journey helping us to let go of the things that hinder our wholeness, a centre where there is space for prayer and meditation and an outward journey focusing on our relationship with the world around us.

• **Prayer walks:** Getting out into the community is a great way to get yourself motivated to pray and to provide visual stimulation to your prayers. For example, as you walk past the doctor's surgery you can pray for all the people with health problems in your area, or, going past a local school, pray for the children, parents and teachers. Perhaps get cell groups to take turns doing a prayer walk each week, or get groups of about three people to sign up. You could break the area up into small chunks and all walk during the same evening,

meeting together at the beginning or end to pray and worship together. Draw maps of routes and put markers along the way with particular things for people to pray for, or let people set their own pace and go where they like.

• **24-7 prayer:** At the start of the year, just before or just after a big event or one of the HOPE 08 high points, you may want to focus your prayer activity and encourage your church, village, town or city to hold a week of 24-7 prayer. 24-7 has been one of the most inspiring prayer movements in recent years whose vision is to 'transform the world through a movement of Christ-centred, mission-minded prayer'. Their website has loads of creative ideas for bringing prayer to life, plus you can get information on how to set up a prayer room, read other people's stories and join the 24-7 community at www.uk.24-7prayer.com.

The young people in your church may like to take the lead in setting up a prayer room.

• **Thanksgiving parties:** Centuries ago, God ordained 'thank-offerings' as part of the Israelites' worship (see Lev. 7:12) and the same truth applies to us today. Prayer is obviously not just about asking for things but thanking God for what he has done. Let's take some time during 2008 to honour God by gathering over a meal to thank him for all that he *has done* for us, all that he *is doing* in the lives of those we are praying for and all that he *will do* in the future. A good opportunity for this is around the dates of the Thanksgiving celebrations in United States of America (Thursday 27 November 2008) and Canada (Monday 13 October 2008). This would also be an ideal time to pray ahead for the Christmas high point (see Chapter 8). A Thanksgiving dinner can involve all age groups, you could have worship and thanks between each course, ask for people to share stories over their food, and focus especially on friends and contacts you want to invite to Christmas celebrations and carol services.

Getting out into the community is a great way to get yourself motivated to pray.

• **Sacred Space** is a resource developed by Bible Society and www.rejesus.co.uk/spirituality/sacred_space designed to help you bring your spirituality into your workplace. The free download has lots of suggestions for individuals, teams and whole companies including ideas for prayer and thanksgiving.

• **Games for children to pray:** If we want our children to be passionate about prayer we need to not only model the importance of prayer in our lives but also find ways that help them engage with God. Games are a great way to do this.

- During a game such as football, basketball or netball whenever a team scores both sides run to the touchline to pick up a prayer topic and instructions to pray briefly before resuming the game;

- Put together an obstacle course so children have to go under tables, over chairs, through hoops, under blankets and in and out of cones. When each person reaches the end they collect a prayer point, bring it back to their team and together they pray for two minutes before the next team member begins the course;

- Ask each child to write a prayer request they are happy to share and put the paper inside a deflated balloon. Blow up all the balloons, play some music and get the children to keep the balloons in the air while the music plays. When it stops, everyone grabs a balloon, bursts it and spends the next few minutes in silent prayer for the request they find inside.

More ideas for encouraging children of all ages to pray are available on our website www.hope08.com.

• **Praying in cell groups:** We don't always have to set up separate meetings to pray; why not just encourage your small groups to take five minutes at the end of their usual meeting to pray for the community and HOPE 08 initiatives?

• **HOPE 08 prayer chains:** As part of our commitment to unity it would be great to have a joined up HOPE prayer chain across villages, towns and cities. When there is a prayer request, each person who is part of the chain should contact the next person on the list and so on, until many people are aware of the issue and praying for its resolve. It's good to also pass thanksgivings back along the chain too so that people are encouraged that their prayers are making a difference.

• **Finding out the prayer needs in your community**

- Place a prayer box somewhere prominent in the community (such as a Post Office, a pub or shop where the management is happy for you to do so), and provide slips of paper for people to leave their prayer requests. Local churches could then pick up the box each week and pray for the requests;

- Or you could drop leaflets to local shops and businesses and ask them to email you with their prayer requests;

- Prayer mapping is where church members each select a street to pray for, then they visit each home and ask for prayer requests.

• **Be inspired by our Christian heritage:** It's inspiring to think about other Christians who have gone ahead of us and literally changed the world around them, playing their part and bringing God's kingdom to earth. Now you can visit historical Christian sites around the UK, walk where some of the heroes of the faith have walked and pray where they have prayed. Visit www.englandschristianheritage.org.uk to find out more about the Christian heritage in your county.

It's inspiring to think about other Christians who have gone ahead of us and literally changed the world around them, playing their part and bringing God's kingdom to earth.

• **Take part in Friday Focus:** During 2007 and 2008, prayer themes for each Friday will be available on www.worldprayer.org.uk by following the Year of Prayer link. Join with many churches, organisations, ministries and individuals praying for these themes each week.

• **Healing rooms:** You may like to explore the idea of opening a healing room, which would offer prayer for healing for anyone in your community, by small teams of trained volunteers. There a number of established healing rooms across the UK – check out www.hope08.com for more details.

• **Prayer on the streets:** If you're sensitive in your approach it can be highly effective to ask people if they would like prayer while they are out and about in a shopping centre etc. Pray for words of knowledge that God might give you insight into things to pray for.

• **Prayer breakfast:** Organise a prayer breakfast for leaders in your community such as MPs, MEPs, local government officials and police. Ask them how you can best pray for them for their role in the community.

• **Individual prayer:** Throughout 2008 we want to encourage personal prayer as well as corporate.

- Praying the Bible: Take passages of Scripture that focus on God's heart for the broken and the marginalised and make them your prayers (such as Is. 58:6–12).

- Praying for your church: At the start of the year write the name of each member of your congregation on a piece of paper and place them in a bowl. Each member then takes one name and commits to praying for that person, their outreach and evangelism that year.

- Write a prayer for HOPE 08: You can share your prayers either on a notice board at your church or on our website www.hope08.com.

- Make a prayer board: Pin names, events, pictures and scriptures to a notice board to act as a visual reminder of all the things you want to commit to God in prayer. If you have a special place where you pray keep it there or have it in a prominent place that you walk past to prompt you to keep praying.

- At 1 p.m. each day, pray for one person for one minute.

Prayers to use

Use the prayers on the HOPE 08 website www.hope08.com or write your own. Share your prayers with others by posting them on the site.

RESOURCES

Websites

www.24-7prayer.com – Find out more about the 24-7 prayer movement, read about prayer and boiler rooms, as well as checking out other people's prayer stories

> Take passages of Scripture that focus on God's heart for the broken and the marginalised and make them your prayers

www.rejesus.co.uk/spirituality - learn to pray, post a prayer, download a prayer, find a sacred space and learn about prayer labyrinths

www.worldprayer.org.uk for Year of Prayer 2007 Friday Focus themes. Email: prayer@worldprayer.org.uk

www.prayerinaction.net

www.40-days.com – includes a free download of a 40 prayer guide produced by There is Hope

www.pray-as-you-go.org – Pray-as-you-go is a daily prayer session, designed for use on portable MP3 players (or computer), to help you pray while travelling. Free to download

www.radiantlight.org.uk – encouragement in the Catholic faith through paintings and meditations

www.waymakers.org – free monthly email prayer guide helping focus prayer for those not following Jesus Christ

www.noonministries.com – NOON (Need Of Our Nation) encourage people to pray for one hour between noon and one o'clock for our nation

www.schoolsprayernetwork.org.uk – prayer for schools

www.healingrooms.com

www.gg2w.org.uk – Getting God to Work

www.when2pray.net – helping couples pray together

www.crossrhythms.co.uk/prayerrooms – add your own prayers at The Incinerator

www.prayer-alert.net – weekly prayer email for national European and world current issues

Books

Prayer – Unwrapping the gift, John Preston. Encouraging the local church to pray with photocopyable prayer resources, including a prayer audit. Published by Authentic Media. £3.50 from www.authenticmedia.co.uk.

Your Kingdom Come, J John. Study guide for home groups on the Lord's Prayer. £3.50 from www.philotrust.com.

Ignite, Nigel James and Carl Brettle. Seven ways to ignite outrageous prayer, Published by Authentic Media. £7.99 from www.authenticmedia.co.uk.

Grove Booklets Spirituality series such as *Simple Tools for Stillness,* Wanda Nash. Available for £2.95 from www.grovebooks.co.uk.

God 360, Andy Flanagan. 120 experiential devotionals, published by Authentic £8.99 from http://store.springharvest.org.

The 24-7 Prayer Manual and CD Rom, published by Kingsway £9.99, order from www.equippingthechurch.co.uk.

Prayerworks – The Manual, 24-7 and Faithworks, Published by Authentic £6.99 from http://store.springharvest.org.

Community Prayer Cells – How to be good news neighbours, Jane Holloway. Church Pastoral Aid Society. £5 from www.cpas.org.uk.

Pocket Prayers for Work, compiled by Mark Greene. £5.99 from www.chpublishing.co.uk.

Prayer can be deeply personal… there are many creative and fun ways to keep praying.

Miscellaneous

• **Saints at Prayer,** Michael Mitton. This course is an ideal resource to teach people to pray in groups with confidence. Available from ReSource, 01235 553922 www.resource-arm.net: £7 Leader's Manual, £4 Link Workbook.

• **Prayer Magazine.** A quarterly, interdenominational publication strengthening Christians, churches and prayer groups across Great Britain and Ireland, featuring articles on HOPE 08. Bulk copies for your church or prayer group from 95p a copy, and individual subscriptions from only £9.99 for one year. To order copies or for further information call 0115 921 7280, email prayer@newlifepublishing.co.uk or visit www.newlifepublishing.co.uk.

• **Purify CD,** Graham Kendrick. A journey of reflection with songs. £3 from www.care.org.uk/shop

• **Ignition cards** help you pray for three friends who aren't Christians. Order free by emailing info@igniteme.org. See www.igniteme.org for more detail.

• **CARE** publish a quarterly prayer diary which will feature HOPE 08 prayer updates – see www.care.org.uk.

CHAPTER 13

HOPE IN THE PUBLIC SPACE

Rob Cotton (Bible Society)

HOPE BILLBOARD MEDIA CAMPAIGN

The gap between our culture and the Bible seems to now be so wide that people need help in engaging with the Bible, the church and the Christian faith. It is no longer true to say that Christianity has been carefully considered by most people and then, on balance, rejected. In the most part, people do not realise that the Bible has something to say about the things that they are dealing with in their daily experiences, or believe that the church has any part to play.

In recent years, Bible Society has run a Media Billboard Campaign in Nottingham, Bristol and Greater Manchester using storylines from the soap EastEnders as a way of getting people to engage with the stories and wisdom of the Bible. Issues of revenge, forgiveness, trust, betrayal, new beginnings and family relationships were explored, with the statement that stories in soaps explore themes first dealt with in the Bible. 'If one grips the nation, why dismiss the other?' Stories were profiled on billboards, bus shelters, bus rears and beer mats using the statement 'Soap Stories and the Bible. Both full of life's struggles, choices and emotions. The Bible more relevant than you thought?'

For any churches that are interested and have available budget, HOPE 08 is a great opportunity

Will Chloe always come between Sonia and Martin?

text: yes chloe or no chloe to 60003
or vote at www.getthestory.co.uk

to take this type of media campaign and roll it out across our villages, towns and cities. Media packages can be developed which suit the needs of your situation and make the most of the opportunities during HOPE 08 to engage the public.

The campaign can help change people's perceptions and facilitate opportunities for conversation and real engagement with the general public. It can connect with the thoughts, feelings, emotions and real lives of people, in such a way that they will be able to consider the relevance of the Bible for themselves.

The media campaign is

• **A way to bring the Bible** to people's attention and prompt them to explore its relevance and significance.
• **An attempt to engage directly** with popular culture, with those who have little or no experience of the church, the Bible or the Christian faith.
• **A way of promoting conversations.**
• **A means of creating a climate of interest** and intrigue around the Bible.
• **An open-ended invitation** for people to explore the Bible's relevance for themselves. The campaign has no prescribed outcome as we believe that when the Bible is unleashed, outcomes cannot be predicted nor should they be controlled.
• **An attempt to get the general public** to consider the Bible's place in their lives.
• **A way of presenting a fresh perspective** on the Bible, the church and the Christian faith.

What it is not

• **An evangelistic mission** in its own right.
• **A campaign aimed** at getting people to read the Bible, attend any church or respond prescriptively. These are welcome outcomes but they are not the prime focus of the campaign.
• **A way of selling** more Bibles or promoting any denomination or particular church.

> The campaign can connect with the thoughts, feelings, emotions and real lives of people.

Bible Society support

Bible Society offers professional expertise, core funding to develop the creative and a focus for mission. Working closely with local church representatives, the campaign will be tailor-made using Bible Society's in-house and freelance staff. We offer a campaign which expresses our organisational values, being passionate, intelligent, pioneering, trustworthy, accountable and professional in all that we do.

If your village, town or city would like to work in partnership with Bible Society to engage today's culture and make the Bible known through a high-profile billboard campaign or showcase event, please contact Revd Rob Cotton, Senior Campaign Manager, to book an appointment and presentation to your church or group of churches. Tel: 07766 075486 or email: rob.cotton@biblesociety.org.uk.

For further information, please see www.biblesociety.org.uk/greatermanchester

CHAPTER 14

HOPE AND YOUR SMALL GROUP

Laurence Singlehurst (Cell UK)

There are three significant ways your small groups or cell group structure can be involved in HOPE 08.

- **Even if your church isn't active in HOPE 08,** your small group could still initiate a number of the ideas and get involved in some of the HOPE 08 high points referred to in this publication.
- **The second, and probably the primary way** that small groups will be involved in HOPE

Small groups are the best place to encourage one another to live out and to do those things that we have committed ourselves to.

08 is as a support to church and projects across the whole of your village, town or city.

Big meetings and church leadership are fantastic at setting a broad agenda and equipping, but small groups are the best place for accountability where, on a week-by-week basis, we encourage one another to live out and to do those things that we have committed ourselves to.

- **The third significant way** that small groups can contribute to HOPE 08 is they become a place where those who have expressed interest in faith throughout the year can become a part of church life. So it is good to think through, during the early part of HOPE 08, how to make your small group/cell group a place to welcome in those who have begun a journey of faith, or whether you could train up a leader who could help start a new small group through Alpha.

GREAT IDEAS

1. In 2007, take a few copies of this publication to your small group/cell group and ask people to read it at an individual level. Encourage people to think about how they are going to be involved then discuss your personal contributions in a small group meeting and think through what you might want to do together.

2. Ongoing prayer. Luke 10:2 tells us that the 'harvest is plentiful' (NIV) but we should pray for the labourers. One way to do this is that at the end of every small group/cell meeting you pray for one person, asking them what the challenges they face at work are, moral dilemmas, pressures and how you can pray for them in their workplace context. Secondly, who have they been called to love? Who are they a secret pastor to (see Chapter 15)? Pray for them to have the love and the wisdom to reach out to their friends. Pray for any particular HOPE 08 initiatives that they are involved in as an individual. This strategy will achieve two things: it is a tremendous encouragement for people to be prayed for and it also involves the whole group in caring for one another. Depending on the size of your group, everyone should get prayed for about once every ten weeks and is encouraged in this personal way.

3. Create a net. Often when we think of mission we think of our personal and individual reaching out to people, 'It's me and my fishing rod.' But it might be much better to think of ourselves as nets; a community of people.

It is a tremendous encouragement for people to be prayed for.

Discuss as a group how you could get to know each other's friends and form a community which includes Christians and non-Christians. In a sense, our small groups now have two dynamics, an inner core which is the Christians meeting together to pray, seek the Lord and encourage one another, and then an outer group who are the friends of the small group and wherever possible we mix our lives together. Perhaps think that every fourth group meeting could be a social event: go bowling, have a meal and invite friends into the life of this little community. What this achieves is, slowly but surely, our non-Christian friends not only see the life of Christ in us but they begin to see it in other people and this is a tremendous way to reinforce our message.

Fun ideas for your cell group to get involved in HOPE 08

- **Hold a barbecue for your cell group and their friends who aren't Christians.**

- **Wash the cars in the neighbourhood where you meet.**

- **Go on a prayer walk of your local neighbourhood together.**

- **Put on a meal for your neighbours or hold a street party.**

- **Encourage each other to get involved in AOK days (see Chapter 15) to commit random Acts of Kindness.**

- **Offer practical help to the friends of your cell group, e.g. if they are moving house or decorating.**

- **Have a barbecue and watch a Euro 2008 football match.**

- **Take over a local curry house for the night and invite your friends to join you.**

- **Turn a wasteland area into a garden.**

- **Raise some money and give it to a local school or charity.**

4. Think growth. As we love people, as individuals and a group, and we sow this love into their lives, at some point some of the people that we care for will respond and will want to begin a journey of faith. So as a group we need to prepare for this moment. We can do this by adding people into our existing group if it is not already too big or we can think of choosing one or two group members who we could equip and empower to start a new group.

Use the *May I call you friend?* resource from the Inter Faith Relations and Evangelism Strategy Groups of the Methodist Church as part of your small group's preparation for HOPE 08. This book addresses the vital questions about how we, as Christians, can share our faith with those of other religions. What is the relationship between dialogue and evangelism? How can people of different faiths work together to serve their communities? These are just some of the issues that are addressed in *May I Call You Friend?*; a resource designed for use by small groups. It contains guidance for discussion about six key subjects: conversion; community action; presence; sharing stories; prayer; worship and listening, and talking about God. The book contains case studies, Bible studies and questions that will provoke vigorous discussion plus a section encouraging the groups to 'turn words into action', providing resources for dialogue and evangelism, including useful websites.
Order for £3.50 from Methodist Publishing House at www.mph.org.uk.

Don't forget to use Burns Night, St David's Day, St Patrick's Day and St Andrew's Day as opportunities to hold celebratory events to invite friends to.

How can people of different faiths work together to serve their communities?

Hope-filled Prayer

Rather than having a separate prayer meeting, why not take five minutes at the end of your cell or small group meeting to pray about your individual, cell/small group and church involvement in the community and any HOPE 08 initiatives you are involved in?

RESOURCES

- **Evangelism Through Cells,** a booklet by Liz West and Laurence Singlehurst, available from Cell UK for £3.50. Tel: 01582 463232.
- **Sowing, Reaping, Keeping,** Laurence Singlehurst. This book helps the reader explore what it means to love people, to sow seeds of faith, to reap the harvest at the right time and to nurture growing faith. Published by Inter-Varsity Press. £6.99 from www.ivpbooks.com.
- **Cell UK** produce a magazine four times a year with inspiring articles and practical ideas for cell leaders. Available via www.celluk.org.uk.

ALOVE+

The Salvation Army for a new generation

Want to see communities transformed?
Want God to transform you?

NEW FOR 2007
£ZERO!!
MAKING YOUR GAP YEAR AFFORDABLE
For the Essential1 programme year beginning September 2007, Training fees have been reduced from £1400 to £0!

ESSENTIAL.1
Discipleship and mission training programme

ESSENTIAL.2
Follow on from ESSENTIAL1 and be trained in your area of vocation

NEO
Be equipped to live, work and serve in some of the toughest estates in the UK and develop new expressions of the church where they are most needed

WHERE WILL IT TAKE YOU?
WHEREVER YOU IMAGINE...

Tel: +44 (0)20 8288 1202
Email: alove.essential@salvationarmy.org.uk
Web: www.salvationarmy.org.uk/alove/essential

CHAPTER 15
BEING A GOOD NEIGHBOUR

Laurence Singlehurst (Cell UK)

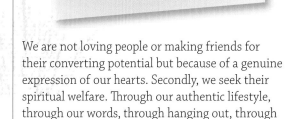

Most Christian research into how people come to faith comes back to one overriding and fundamental statistic – that at least 70 per cent have been helped along in that process by a friendship with a Christian. This same research points out that most non-Christians need at least seven or eight positive interactions with Christianity before they are ready to go on an Alpha course or give their lives to Christ in a significant way.

Our clear conclusion is that as local churches we need to use friendship as the fundamental basis of evangelism. A word of warning: this must not be a strategy; rather, it needs to be an expression of love, therefore our friendship-based evangelism should begin with asking God for big hearts.

Ed Silvoso introduced a metaphor that I think helps us to see friendship evangelism in a new way. He encouraged every Christian to think of themselves as a secret pastor with a congregation made up of non-Christians. I have added to that two further thoughts. Firstly, we must love people unconditionally, regardless of whether they respond or not.

> This must not be a strategy; it needs to be an expression of love.

We are not loving people or making friends for their converting potential but because of a genuine expression of our hearts. Secondly, we seek their spiritual welfare. Through our authentic lifestyle, through our words, through hanging out, through sitting in smoke-filled rooms we express our care and love and speak the words when the opportunities arise.

Hospitality is a theme right the way through the Bible from Old Testament to New Testament and is one of the best ways to reach out. It is such an important theme because it is a heart response to the value of people and it is such a dynamic interaction. Inviting people into your home to have a cup of tea, a meal or to watch a football game has always spoken to people and always will.

In seeking to be good neighbours we want to become very hospitable people.

What does being a friend achieve? In friendship we give people an opportunity to see their stereotype of God and Christians broken down. Sadly, a great percentage of our nation has a fairly negative view of God and an even more negative view of us. We are seen as boring. No, not just boring, but very boring, and through friendship we create a foundation to change that. The first step on a journey of faith must be that God is good and we are OK. This foundation is essential and then from there people might begin to respond, ask questions, want to go to Alpha etc. A friend of mine has been playing golf with his friend for seven years. For five of those seven years this friend has shown very little interest in Christianity but suddenly in the last year he has begun to ask questions and is currently on an Alpha course. This is about the long haul which is why our friendships must be genuine or they won't make it.

GREAT IDEAS

So let us consider some practical ways to put this into action.

1. Evangelism starts with a big heart so as early as possible in 2008 use a Sunday meeting or a prayer meeting to get the church to ask God for big hearts, that we would see the true value of those around us.

The first step on a journey of faith must be that God is good and we are OK.

2. Share the concept of being a secret pastor. Encourage every church member to have a small congregation, maybe two people where they live, three people at work, or four people they hang out with, it doesn't really matter. If we all ask God for a congregation, however small or big, and put the principles of being a secret pastor into action, we will be making an impact.

3. Sometime in 2007, preach a Sunday morning message on hospitality, look at some of the Old Testament and New Testament references and put the thought out there that we all need to be more hospitable.

4. Get hold of the Tearfund 'The Good Neighbours Pack' (www.tearfund.org. Tel: 0845 355 8355 or email enquiry@tearfund.org). This straightforward and fun guide enables churches and small groups to explore the 'hows' of being a good neighbour, i.e. how do you get to know your neighbour when you don't even know their name? How do you get to know your neighbour better when you don't see them very often? And how do you get to know neighbours when they are so different from you? Using games and brainstorming activities the pack helps you come up with easy, practical ways to get more friendly with your neighbours, build relationships and be a blessing to them.

5. Consider joining something in your community that gives you a greater link to that community, for example, join the golf club or local football team, become a regular at a local pub, join the amateur dramatics group or historical society, hang out on the skateboarding ramp or learn to dance – whatever is your interest. Remember, stay authentic (or people will see right through you) but be involved.

6. Find out more about how you could get involved with Street Pastors, an inter-denominational church response to urban problems. Street Pastors spend time on the streets during the hours of 10 p.m. to around 4 a.m. engaging with people who are out and about at that time,

listening to their problems and caring for them. Training is provided – see our Case Study and www.streetpastors.org.uk for more information.

7. Party, party! We all love parties so why not encourage every church member to have a birthday party this year where they invite their Christian and non-Christian friends? Push the boat out, have some fun, and include into that fun any non-Christians you and your friends know.

8. Take a value to work. In the workplace, lifestyle and attitude speaks volumes and one of the ways that we can fulfil our salt and light mandate is to think of a Christian value that we can embrace for ourselves and take to work. Part of the great commandment is you should love your neighbour as yourself which speaks very powerfully of having a high value of people. This is a good passage to speak from at some point in the life of a church; encourage church members to think through what that might look like. For example, one businessman, on taking this value to work, realised that there were a lot of support staff outside his office who he just did not know though they had been there for many years. He started to greet them by name on his way through and sent flowers to any who were sick and slowly but surely changed that little bit of his work space.

The kingdom of God had come to the fifth floor. See www.rejesus.co.uk/spirituality (Sacred Space) for creative ideas for the workplace.

9. Invite your neighbours to a course such as Alpha in your house. Many courses have videos or DVDs you can use which work well in small groups. See Chapter 7 for more information about courses.

Getting started

It would be ideal to prepare for this in 2007 so that in 2008, individuals begin to think of being a secret pastor and identify who their congregations are, both at work and in their locality. This strategy then links well with the HOPE 08 high point later on in the year where churches are encouraged to be

Join the golf club or local football team, become a regular at a local pub, join the amateur dramatics group or historical society, hang out on the skateboarding ramp or learn to dance.

involved in Alpha or a similar project in September/October (see Chapter 7). A few of the people that are in church members' congregations may be open to come to an Alpha-like project, or a Christmas carol service or event. Hopefully it will be possible for church members to invite all of the local people that they are now a secret pastor to, to one of these events.

Hope-filled Prayer

Make your home a 'house of prayer'; a place where you pray for your neighbours, your street, your community, your family, friends and home group. Let people know they can always come to your house and ask for prayer.

Southend Street Life

LOVE SOUTHEND is an inter-church, borough-wide initiative which seeks to reveal the love which God has, for every Southender, through acts of generosity and social-concern.

One vital aspect of LOVE SOUTHEND is the work of our Street Pastors. Made up of volunteers from various local congregations, the Pastors are out and about in Southend clubland and partyland, every Friday and Saturday night. They go, not so much to preach at people, but as an unobtrusive Christian presence, through being a listening ear or a friendly, welcoming face in often cold, hostile streets.

In our first two years, LOVE SOUTHEND Street Pastors has engaged with almost five thousand people. Many of these have led to interesting, meaningful conversations. A few people have asked for prayer, but many encounters are much more earthly. Some Pastors have supplied blankets and soup to those sleeping rough, some have administered first aid or cleared vomit from people's faces. What's more, they've also diffused a good number of potential fights through bravely talking with people – and a bit of emergency prayer. On the streets and in the clubs, through the amusement arcades and at the Bowling Alley, the Pastors are well received and many people know about them and their motivations. Indeed, the Pastors are often thanked for just being there and for tangibly helping to improve the atmosphere on the street.

LOVE SOUTHEND Street Pastors now work in close connection with the SOS Bus in the town centre. They use an SOS Bus radio to communicate when they're bringing a 'guest' along to the bus – or when they need the Bus crew's assistance. Recently, they've called for the nurse who arrived in a dedicated mobile vehicle, administered treatment and therefore avoided the need to call ambulances and clog up Casualty.

People have asked for prayer. Pastors have supplied blankets and soup to those sleeping rough, some have administered first aid or cleared vomit from people's faces.

LOVE SOUTHEND Street Pastors enjoy the support of a dedicated team of prayer supporters back at base at Clarence Road Baptist Church. The Pastors are out from 10 p.m.– 4.00 a.m., and the prayer team are constantly praying for their protection and for the protection of those whom they encounter.

Local MP James Dudderidge said, 'It really is encouraging to know that there are people in Southend who are passionate about the welfare of our community and who are willing to work all hours to achieve it.'

www.streetpastors.org.uk

RESOURCES

- *Sowing, Reaping, Keeping,* Laurence Singlehurst. This book helps the reader explore what it means to love people, to sow seeds of faith, to reap the harvest at the right time and to nurture growing faith. Published by Inter-Varsity Press. £6.99 from www.ivpbooks.com.
- *Angels on your doorstep,* Paddy Beresford. Published by Kingsway. £6.99 from www.equippingthechurch.co.uk.
- **If you would value support in your workplace,** the opportunity to talk to other Christians about the pressures and problems you face, or just want to feel encouraged in your efforts to bring God's kingdom to your work why not consider joining Bands? These small groups meet in workplaces around the country, offering support and friendship – find out more at www.citybands.co.uk.
- **Being a Christian in the workplace** – www.gg2w.org.uk
- **Community Prayer Cells** – *How to be good news neighbours,* Jane Holloway. Church Pastoral Aid Society. £5 from www.cpas.org.uk.

Why not get involved in an AOK day? This initiative from Soul Action is about making Fridays a day when young people across the country undertake random Acts of Kindness (hence the AOK!). Soul Action will come up with the ideas and post them on their website each week – www.soulaction.org or you can sign up to have them emailed to you. All you have to do is log on and then make those around you smile with your AOK!

DANCE TO A DIFFERENT BEAT

IT COULD CHANGE YOUR WORLD. WE'LL EQUIP YOU TO PRAY WITH PASSION, CAMPAIGN FOR JUSTICE AND TAKE ACTION ON BEHALF OF THE POOR. CHANGE THE WAY YOU LIVE YOUR LIFE FOR GOOD, FOR OTHERS, FOREVER. CONTACT TEARFUND TO FIND OUT HOW. YOUR MAGAZINE, YOUR WEBSITE, YOUR LIFESTYLE. MAKE YOUR MOVE.

CONNECT: www.tearfund.org/youth **CLICK:** enquiry@tearfund.org
CALL: 0845 355 8355 (ROI: 00 44 845 355 8355)

TEARFUND

CHRISTIAN ACTION WITH THE WORLD'S POOR

115647 Registered Charity No. 265464

'A million hours of kindness can be interpreted in so many creative ways; it will be an exhilarating and inspiring year.'

'HOPE 08 is a wonderful initiative and an opportunity for local churches throughout the country to work in their communities and make a real difference to their neighbours.'

planning
and preparing

'Be good news
in practical
and tangible
ways that bring
wholeness and
liberation.'

CHAPTER 16

WORKING WITH THE POLICE, GOVERNMENT AND THE MEDIA

Matt Bird (Make It Happen)

POLICE AND GOVERNMENT

Over recent years there has been a greater recognition from government about the significant contribution of churches, synagogues, mosques and faith-based charities to community life, with those who have a faith being far more likely to volunteer and have an altruistic involvement in their local community. While this is the general trend there are some people within government who are nervous about working with faith-based organisations, particularly if they are seen to favour Christianity as the majority faith (the last census showed that 71 per cent of the UK population describe themselves as Christian). It is good to make it clear that our churches are 'faith based but not faith biased' and therefore serve people of all faiths and none, but what drives us to engage is our faith in Jesus Christ. If that faith is somehow suppressed or denied than it is like uncoupling the engine from the train and still expecting the carriages to move.

There are significant benefits to working with police and government:

> Our churches are 'faith based but not faith biased' and therefore serve people of all faiths and none.

- **The Bible tells us** that no authority exists except that which God has ordained so working with local police and government is a great opportunity to *collaborate* with God's purposes.
- **Police and government** have significant *knowledge* about local communities and expertise about working in them and they are always keen to work with other community stakeholders.
- **Working in partnership** with local police and government can offer *credibility* with other partners, community stakeholders and the local media (more on this later in this chapter).
- **Working together** with local police and government is always primarily about partnership but they also have *financial resources* that can be granted to local groups doing something that assists them in meeting their targets.

Do remember that local police and government have very different and distinctive cultures and ways of working. The police have a very strong command and control culture, which means that when the senior officer says something should happen, it usually does. Local government is expected to act in a manner which is directly accountable to local people through political leadership and also to central government. This can create a bureaucratic culture which can be as frustrating for those who work there as for people attempting to work in partnership with them.

HOPE 08 has agreed with the police nationally (Association of Chief Police Officers,

Neighbourhood Policing Programme) a set of principles for best practice partnership as follows:

1. Engagement and initiatives with neighbourhood police teams and officers will be overseen by local church leaders working in partnership.

2. Churches will work collaboratively to an agreed plan of action and appoint a liaison person responsible for communications with the police neighbourhood team or officer.

3. Church and police partnership activity will be focused on working together in practical ways to benefit the local community and assist current police neighbourhood priorities.

4. Any engagement that involves reducing offending should be co-ordinated with the police and should consider the need for their expert advice.

5. Churches should take a pragmatic approach and acknowledge that police officers will have many conflicting priorities. The value of working together is in shared priorities and outcomes. Churches must recognise there will be occasions when the neighbourhood police team may not be able to support their issues as fully as they might wish.

Church and police partnership activity will be focused on working together in practical ways to benefit the local community.

Who can help?

The following are a selection of organisations that will help you connect with your community, and examples of ways you can put this into practice.

Organisations

1. Redeeming Our Communities – Prayer and Policing in Partnership for Crime Reduction.

Redeeming Our Communities is about seeing community transformation through prayer and policing in partnership by encouraging and informing individuals and small groups to engage with their community and see prayer and action work together. Find out more at www.citylinks.org.uk.

2. Use the 'Adopt-a-Cop' scheme, run by the Christian Police Association, to build links in prayer with your local police. Go to www.cpauk.net for more details.

3. Following the Local Government Act 2000, most local authorities established a partnership (known as a Local Strategic Partnership), which in many places includes a faith representative. When you wish to make contact with your local authority, do speak to the faith representative on the LSP who may be able to help you by directing you to the contacts that he/she has developed.

4. The Lighthouse provide alternative education for excluded young people for the local authority. The Lighthouse Group works with young people who are in crisis in their education because they have been excluded or are at risk of exclusion from school. TLG works closely with schools and local authorities, aiming to tackle the issues that underpin behavioural difficulties and develop learning skills leading to qualifications and a bright future. Currently they are developing centres in partnership with churches in cities in the UK, so why not in your community? See www.thelighthousegroup.co.uk.

5. Street Pastors is a project working on the streets and bars, pubs and clubs to reduce anti-social behaviour at night-time. The Ascension Trust Street Pastors is a partnership between local church, police and government to tackle night-time anti-social behaviour and crime. Teams of Street Pastors who are fully trained volunteers work on the streets and bars, pubs and clubs to be a reassuring presence.

See www.streetpastors.org.uk and the Case Study in Chapter 15 for more details.

6. The Trussell Trust's FOOD BANK is an innovative project for the church to provide essential food and nutrition to people in crisis. They provide short term, nutritionally balanced, emergency food to individuals and families in crisis through a network of churches working with local authority social services. For example, in one year, the Salisbury FOOD BANK collected over 60,000 tins and packets and fed three days supply of food to 2,814 people as well as 1,200 meals to rough sleepers and 1,000 meals to people in hostels in their local community. The FOOD BANK is being developed in villages, towns and cities around the country so why not take the initiative in yours?

See www.trusselltrust.org.

Examples of good practice

• **London Week of Peace** – a project engaging local people of all faiths, and schools, youth groups, community and voluntary groups to encourage peace and reconciliation within communities. The Peace Alliance has developed the week of peace within communities, which is a festival celebrating and promoting community peace and reconciliation. In particular the week of peace has built good relations between faith communities. An initiative of this nature in your community has the potential to receive significant involvement from local police and government.

See www.peacealliance.org.uk.

• **The SNAC** (Safer Neighbourhoods Annual Challenge) – a local police project working with groups of young people in the local community. It is the initiative of a Christian police officer

Remember the media are not there to promote causes... but they are always interested in reporting objectively good local interest stories.

to challenge groups of young people to identify a problem within their neighbourhood, suggest solutions to these problems, and then act to make those answers work. This project has now become an annual event with a public award ceremony for the best projects. SNAC resources are now available for use within any community. See www.thesnac.com.

WORKING WITH THE MEDIA

Working with the media provides a great opportunity to raise awareness of the work you are doing in your local community. Here are some helpful points to remember and an action plan:

• **Remember** the media are not there to promote causes through free advertising but they are always interested in reporting objectively good local interest stories.

• **Identify or create** your story. Consider what the church is doing through HOPE 08 and create an event that can be reported on such as a project opening ceremony, a special finale, an awards ceremony or simply the visit of a special guest. The involvement of a special guest can provide extra interest for the media if for example it is your local Member of Parliament or perhaps a local celebrity.

• **Get to know your local press.** Pick up copies of the local paper/s in your newsagents, collect the copies of the free press that come through the door and tune in to local and regional radio stations. In addition, The Newspaper Society provides an excellent website database providing contact information on daily, weekly and monthly publications at www.newspapersoc.org.uk/ISBA-maps/weekly-maps.htm and the BBC provides a list of its regional radio services at www.bbc.co.uk/.

• **Build a list** of local and regional media contacts, and particularly email addresses as that is the easiest and quickest way to get your stories and pictures to the right place. It is also very useful to have telephone numbers, as picking up the phone to a news editor will also be important.

- **It is best to draft** the press release prior to the event and then you can tweak the details or story slightly after the event. It is important to get your press release in the hands of the media as soon as possible after the event. Please see 'How to write a press release' below.

- **A day after you have sent your press release,** pick up the phone to the news editor or pop into the office to confirm they have received it. The more you can build a positive rapport with the newspaper or radio station, the more likely they are to look favourably at your stories. If they use your story, remember to thank them.

- **It may be that you would like to invite** local and regional media to attend your event. This can be advantageous as they may send a photographer who will take a professional shot (if they do make sure you assign someone to look after them to make them feel welcome). However, news editors are always on tight deadlines and things can crop up last minute so don't build your hopes on this too much. If they don't make it to the event, a press release after the event will do the job.

> The more you can build a positive rapport with the newspaper or radio station, the more likely they are to look favourably at your stories.

How to write a press release

- FORMAT – Use a single A4 page, double space the lines, use size 11 or 12 font. If, when you have written the press release, it is longer than you thought and you are tempted to use more than one page, use 1.5 space for the lines and/or use a smaller font – please do not simply cut out important text.

- DATE – State the date clearly at the top of the page.

- HEADING – At the top of the page write a very short and punchy heading for the story. The heading should be underlined, in bold and upper case.

- The first paragraph should provide a clear introduction concisely describing the who, what, where, when and why of the story.

- The further three of four paragraphs should flesh out the story and provide a quote from someone who is involved in the project.

- Remember to avoid using Christian jargon.

To see a sample press release go to www.hope08.com

GREAT IDEAS

Working with the media

1. Make your story about local people. Demonstrate the benefit for a particular group of local people in your project such as young people, the elderly or single parents.

2. Celebrities. Involve a local celebrity or public figure such as a Member of Parliament in your project or programmes event as this will provide the media with another point of interest in your story.

3. KISS – 'Keep It Simple Stupid!' Decide what your simple key message or messages to the media are and stick to your script.

4. Photocalls. Set up a photograph opportunity for the local media that involves an interesting group of people, in an interesting place, doing something interesting!

5. Statistics. Link in your story to any local or regional statistics that demonstrate the community need you are addressing, such as the fact that youth crime rates are high as kids are bored in the holidays so you're running a youth initiative for them.

6. Community Questionnaire. You could run a very simple community survey in order to gain some figures on what people think about particular issues or situations. This gives you the headline for your story, for example '77 per cent of local people are concerned about the lack of activities for young people'.

7. If you have experience in radio broadcasting, have been involved in a RSL (a Restricted Service Licence that runs for 28 days), have good relationships with local churches and the wider community, then you are ideally placed to provide a strategic radio voice into your area as part of HOPE 08. Throughout the year we anticipate short term (one month) radio stations popping up across the country, profiling all the great HOPE initiatives taking place, and being strategic HOPE initiatives in their own right! Radio HOPE will be supported and co-ordinated by our friends at Cross Rhythms. For the past five years Cross Rhythms have been delivering an FM community radio station in Stoke-on-Trent and they are now multiplying their unique model with groups in other cities across the UK. With their experience in local community radio, that engages with both the church and the wider community, they will be able to offer loads of support to those who want to take on their own Radio HOPE in 2008. If you're interested send an email to jonathan.bellamy@crossrhythms.co.uk and check out the Cross Rhythms radio station at www.crossrhythms.co.uk to get a feel of the kind of station you may be able to run.

8. Produce HOPE radio ads for your local station. As part of your local HOPE campaign why not build in radio exposure across your city or region? In 2007 let everyone know that HOPE is coming soon and in 2008 let them know how HOPE has arrived in your area! In conjunction with Cross Rhythms, HOPE 08 is producing a series of radio ads ready for use on your local commercial station. Why not budget in a radio awareness campaign? For more details contact info@hope08.com.

As part of your local HOPE campaign why not build in radio exposure across your city or region?

RESOURCES

- **The Faithworks Local Media Guide** – a beginner's guide designed to help churches and Christian community projects make the most of local media. See www.faithworks.info for more information or email info@faithworks.info.

- **How to be Heard in a Noisy World,** Phil Creighton. Whether it's improving the notice board, maximising the effect of the Sunday experience, or sending the right information to your local paper, Phil Creighton has the answers. Packed with cost-effective tips and advice, this covers every aspect of church communication and will help you move forward with confidence. £8.99 from www.authenticmedia.co.uk.

TEARFUND SOULSURVIVOR

SOULACTION
GO:LOCAL

A CD–ROM PACKED FULL OF INFO ON DOING
JESUS CENTRED COMMUNITY ACTION
IN YOUR LOCAL AREA!

INCLUDES PRACTICAL
ADVICE ON...

→ THE NOISE
→ SO
→ C

PL

wholeLIFE   wholeHEART

Soul Action,
Unit 2,
Paramount
Industrial
Estate,
Sandown
Road, Watford,
WD24 7XF

www.soulaction.org
info@soulaction.org.

TEARFUND SOUL SURVIVOR
SOULACTION
wholeHEART wholeLIFE wholeWORLD

Soul Action operates as an
aspect of the work of Soul
Survivor.

The Soul Survivor registered
charity number is 1080720

LOCAL

GETTING SERIOUS ABOUT LOVING YOUR NEIGHBOUR?

SO ARE WE.

Learn how to get you and your church socially active, or scale up what you're already doing, with GO:LOCAL, a CD ROM packed full of info on doing Jesus centred community action in your local area.

This great resource includes all you need to serve your community, from small projects like THE NOISE to town wide events like SOUL IN THE CITY.

It will show you how to prepare your people, connect to your community and plan your programme. Plus through the CD ROM you'll get access to online downloads, forums and regular updates about Soul Action locally and globally.

Check **WWW.SOULACTION.ORG** for more information.

CHAPTER 17
ENGAGING WITH YOUR COMMUNITY

Jon Kuhrt and David Arscott (Shaftesbury Society), Julian Richards, GWEINI (The council for the Christian voluntary sector in Wales)

WHAT IS COMMUNITY MISSION?

Community mission is the active involvement of Christians in their local communities, living out God's kingdom through addressing the needs around us. Community mission brings words and actions together and seeks personal and social transformation – to be good news in practical and tangible ways that bring wholeness and liberation. Community mission takes seriously Micah's call to '...act justly, and to love mercy and to walk humbly with your God' (Mich. 6:8, NIV) and Jesus' instruction to seek first the kingdom of God.

Community mission is the active involvement of Christians in their local communities.

THE COMMUNITY MISSION JOURNEY

The community mission journey is a model developed through experience with partner churches to give an overview of how to get involved in your community and be effective in making a difference. It is best used by a group who are working through how they can make a difference in their community.

It introduces three basic steps:

1. PREPARING FOR ACTION

2. ENGAGING AND RESEARCHING YOUR COMMUNITY

3. EXPLORING MODELS OF ACTION

This tool will help you to identify and consider the options and alert you to the issues you will encounter. It will help you explore the *why, what, when, where and how* of your involvement. It emphasises the importance of listening, working with others, finding out about the needs in your community and responding appropriately.

Step 1: PREPARING FOR ACTION

It is important to explore the question *why should we be involved in our communities?* In the Bible there are many examples to learn from, both in the Old Testament and in the life of Jesus and the early church and you can see Chapter 3 for more on the theology of word and deed mission.

It is *best to prepare for action with others*: in your congregation, among your friends and with people from other local congregations. Find out what motivates you. Do you have enough in common to work together? Do you have similar values? Community mission is hard work and often quite messy. By *sharing motivations* at the start you will find it much easier to overcome problems and confusion later. By having *clear goals* you will be able to plan your work much more easily and be able to clearly identify the real results.

Be committed to praying for your community. Work out what God is saying; what are his concerns for your community? Do a prayer walk, read the local newspapers, listen to local radio and talk to local people to find out what's going on.

Step 2: ENGAGING AND RESEARCHING YOUR COMMUNITY

This step is essential if you want to respond to the key needs in your community, rather than just the needs which are most apparent to you. Although it can be time consuming, researching your community's needs will reap huge benefits in the long run. There are three main sources of information to consult, all of which are equally important:

- Individuals and groups in the community.
- Other agencies and organisations already working in the area.
- Reports and statistics that have already been produced.

> Researching your community's needs will reap huge benefits.

Step 3: EXPLORING MODELS OF ACTION

Now that you know the key needs of the community, you can explore ways in which they may be addressed. It is much better to do one or two things well than to get involved in lots of things without much commitment; you should be aiming for long-term commitment, not 'hit and run' projects, as it is very frustrating for people who begin to rely on a project only to find it has closed down.

Take time to decide the best way to respond to your community's needs, based on the resources and skills you have available. Continue to talk, to pray and seek God's direction for the next steps.

People in your group may not decide on a collective course of action but may agree to support each other in different areas. If you are working with a whole congregation, remember that not everyone needs to work in the same way, and this could give a chance for everyone to use their different gifts.

1. PREPARING FOR ACTION

2. ENGAGING AND RESEARCHING YOUR COMMUNITY

3. EXPLORING MODELS OF ACTION

Getting involved in what's already going on

Campaigning for justice

Social enterprise

Setting up a community project

> Speak out about the underlying issues or causes of injustice that directly affect people's lives.

of a school or campaigning for funding for older people's services. It involves speaking out about the underlying issues or causes of injustice that directly affect people's lives, and co-ordinates people to address the issues together. It may mean taking a lead in identifying official bodies and bringing them together with local people to collaborate in finding solutions.

For more ideas please see:

- **Church Action on Poverty's** website www.church-poverty.org.uk.
- **Speak's** website www.speak.org.uk.
- **Tearfund** offer campaign information on issues such as Fairtrade and climate change. See the campaigning section of www.tearfund.org.

SOCIAL ENTERPRISE

A social enterprise is a business with the primary aim of bringing positive change to the community, such as a local café incorporating training for unemployed people. It may encourage local people in the development of their social economy by building local relationships through the business.

For more information please contact:

- **Pecan,** a Christian organisation working in south London who deliver a range of social enterprises – www.pecan.org.uk.

SETTING UP A COMMUNITY PROJECT

There are a huge range of options and ideas when it comes to setting up a community project. Churches and Christian groups have a long track record of establishing projects to serve the needs of young people, older people and families, as well as those affected by homelessness, debt, disability and mental illness. The government and other agencies such as the police believe that there is a great role for the church

GETTING INVOLVED IN WHAT'S ALREADY GOING ON

Having researched local needs, you will discover many groups and organisations already working in your area. Rather than setting up a separate project, how about getting involved in different initiatives that are already happening? This may be with other Christian congregations, other faith groups, voluntary agencies or statutory agencies. This allows you to work alongside others with similar motivations and passions, to get involved in activities outside your local congregation, and also avoids duplicating existing services. This can be a sacrificial approach as it means laying aside our own agendas to serve other people's visions.

CAMPAIGNING FOR JUSTICE

Campaigning can take place at a local, regional or national level in a response to the specific needs in your local community, such as opposing the closure

in establishing projects and are often very keen to work closely with churches (see Chapter 16). This brings both opportunities and challenges. We believe the important thing is for the church to be clear about what it is trying to achieve, to review progress regularly and to work hard to maintain the Christian distinctiveness of the work.

For more information please see:

- **The Faithworks Best Practice Guide.**
  How to apply Christian faith and values in the day-to-day running of your project, ensuring integrity, transparency and trust.
  See www.faithworks.info.

- **Managing Social Action Projects,**
  produced by the Baptist Union of Great Britain.
  Email baptistuniongb@baptist.org.uk or tel: 01235 517 700.

THREE KEY THEMES
Theme 1: Community development

An overview of Community Development by Julian Richards, GWEINI (The council for the Christian voluntary sector in Wales).

The principles of community development make me think of Proverbs 19:2: 'Enthusiasm without knowledge is not good. If you act too quickly, you might make a mistake' (NCV). Or as Roger, a community activist I came into contact with, said, 'To set up a project without asking if the community want it is immoral.'

Community development is very big right now. Government is investing millions in it and importantly local communities are taking ownership of both the challenges and solutions that local communities face. Residents, charities, statutory bodies, churches and businesses are working in partnership together in an unprecedented way. This new wave of participation has raised the profile of the voluntary sector to such significance that it is now increasingly being called the 'third sector', next to government and business. The implication of this is that community work, or doing acts of kindness in a corporate or organised way in one's local community, now

Gone are the days when we can simply see a need, or think of a project and get on and do our own thing.

demands a little more consideration. Gone are the days when we can simply see a need, or think of a project and get on and do our own thing. Why is that? Because we may, with all the best intentions, be stepping on many toes and offend the very people we are trying to bless through our good works.

As we plan for HOPE 08, here are some key principles to help you as you develop an effective strategy of community engagement.

1. Be prepared to get involved long-term both in relationships and in projects you set up, as people need time to discover, understand and process the message and claims of the gospel. The challenge for us with HOPE 08 is to use the year of 2008 as a starting place, a springboard into a long-haul strategy of engagement and involvement in our local communities that extends way into the future. If we do this, the church will once again become integral to community life and an effective change agent.

2. Consult with your community. People don't want to be told what they need or should have done for them. Consulting with the community will ensure your project is something that is needed and wanted and will be a great starting point for you to meet people and prove your church's willingness to serve. It doesn't have to be complicated but could involve a questionnaire in the streets or in homes; visiting the local youth clubs and asking questions; an interview with head teachers, the police, the local health visitor, councillors, shop owners, local authority officers involved in community development, or the local housing office. It is also advisable to make an appointment to visit other organisations and charities currently working in the area.

3. Develop partnership with others who are working in the community. Partnership is not merger and losing our distinctiveness, even if we join with secular organisations. It is about strategising and talking together, sharing resources where possible, and not duplicating one another's projects. It avoids competition, ensures best value for money where there is funding, and the best possible service for beneficiaries. Working with others also increases our credibility in the community, and the presence of the project we are working on.

Action points:

• **Telephone your local authority** and ask to speak to someone responsible for community development in your area.

• **Ask to meet with your local councillor** and explain your desire to serve your community and get involved.

• **Contact your local council** for voluntary service (CVS or CVC/CVA) and ask who to contact in your area concerning development. Are there any community development groups in your area?

CVCs, or councils for voluntary action, are local umbrella organisations working on behalf of the voluntary sector in a given area. They are a fount of information, very helpful and excellent for advice regarding community work and how to go about it. They also put on a wide range of courses for charities and voluntary organisations. Any organisation, including churches, can join for a very small fee and benefit from their help and expertise.

For more information:

• **See Shaftesbury's booklet,** *Mystery in the Ordinary* – the story of the Shaftesbury Centre in Eastbourne which focuses on putting community development into practice. For copies, call 0845 330 6033

Theme 2: Church working together

Responding to the needs of a community is best done together. There will be a number of different congregations in your community, be it citywide or a local neighbourhood. Agreeing to work together with a focus on the community, across denominations, leads to sharing resources e.g. experience, buildings, volunteers and funding. This enables the church to become much more effective in tackling the effects of deprivation in

> Working with others also increases our credibility in the community, and the presence of the project we are working on.

> 'How relevant are our church activities to people's day-to-day lives?' 'Is this good news for the poor?'

a given area. It motivates congregations to explore what they have in common and work together for the sake of their communities. It can be a powerful witness in the community, demonstrating unity through action, and challenges the view that churches are only concerned with their own growth.

For more information:

• **See Shaftesbury's** website www.challengingchurch.net for many ideas and resources to build unity through community action.

Theme 3: New ways of being church in the community

Community mission can challenge our understanding of church. We may find ourselves with questions such as: 'How relevant are our church activities to people's day-to-day lives?' 'Is this good news for the poor?' 'What is church?' This can be confusing and disruptive but it can also positively lead to a shift in focus, to new ways of being church in the community.

In what ways can we be 'salt and light' in our area? Some Christians choose to go and live in urban areas affected by deprivation and endeavour to build relationships with the community in a natural, organic way. This approach may involve groups of Christians living communally or in different homes within an area for example: 5 Christian households in several streets, who meet to pray for neighbours, share their resources and respond to local needs.

For more information:

• **See the two Fresh Expressions DVDs** for inspiration and examples of what is happening across the UK, 'Stories of church from a changing culture' and 'Changing church in every place'. Fresh Expressions, with a number of other agencies, are also establishing a one-year part-time regional training programme called Mission Shaped Ministry – ideal for teams beginning fresh expressions of church. Visit www.emergingchurch.info or www.freshexpressions.org.uk.

• **ReSource run courses** exploring the mission and practice of church planting in fresh, culturally relevant ways. Find out more at www.resourcechurchplanting.com or by emailing info@resourcechurchplanting.com.

• Be inspired by groups such as Eden who have gone to live in the most difficult areas in order to reach the people there. See www.message.org.uk for more details.

Hope-filled Prayer

Find out the prayer needs in your community by placing a prayer box in a prominant place or by doing a leaflet drop telling people they can email or call with any prayer requests.

> It's vital to go to where people are, listen to their culture, to love and to serve them.

Developing new forms of church

In the last decade across the UK, Christians have been discovering that it's often not enough to make contact with people and invite them to come to church as we know it. It's also vital to go to where people are, listen to their culture, to love and to serve them. As part of that loving service, new communities will begin to form, providing opportunities to share faith and make new disciples. The best way to nurture those disciples may be to begin a new Christian community – a new church – where they are, to reach out to a particular network or culture.

This kind of movement is already happening in thousands of different places. The Church of England and the Methodist Church call these new beginnings 'fresh expressions of church' and elsewhere they are known as 'emerging churches'. There is a big overlap with the church-planting movement, with these new congregations and communities growing up alongside traditional congregations in what the Archbishop of Canterbury has called a 'mixed economy of churches'.

As you think and pray towards HOPE 08, allow your vision to be stretched even beyond loving service and offering the gospel and an invitation to church as it is. Catch a vision for establishing new Christian communities all across the land – fresh expressions of church which can grow and be a means of grace for those beginning the Christian journey.

More details from the fresh expressions website (www.freshexpressions.org.uk) or www.emergingchurch.info or www.encountersontheedge.info.

RESOURCES

Prepare for action

• **Shaftesbury's *Why Social Action?*,** a series of four Bible studies, will help you to develop strong biblical foundations for any community action. Also our *Prayer – Action – Reflection* Cycle helps give a model of action to use on your journey. See www.shaftesburysociety.org.

• **Faithworks** produce a Church Audit Pack to evaluate your church and its potential to rise to the challenge of effective, sustainable community development. They also have a DVD for small groups which includes questions and Bible passages to help your church to think about how you can serve your wider community. See *ichurch: Intelligent Church in the 21st Century* from www.faithworks.info.

• **The Naked Church,** produced by GWEINI (the council for the Christian voluntary sector in Wales) addresses the opportunities and challenges facing Christian welfare initiatives in Wales today providing an invaluable introduction to community development principles for churches everywhere. £4.95 from www.gweini.org.uk.

• **'Expressions: the DVD 1'.** Stories of church for a changing culture. Skater church... cell church... messy church... All over the country Christians are beginning new initiatives to connect with those who are currently outside church. This DVD contains 15 stories of these fresh expressions and describes some of the lessons learned so far. £12.99 from www.chpublishing.co.uk.

• **'Expressions: the DVD 2'.** Changing church in every place. Fresh expressions are flourishing in all types of places ... where you live, worship and work. All over the country Christians are beginning new initiatives to connect with those who are currently outside church. Presented by Diane Louise Jordan, this DVD focuses on four specific areas where fresh expressions of church are breaking new ground. Each film looks at fresh expressions with a distinct focus: sacramental, youth, rural, and work and leisure. £14.99 from www.chpublishing.co.uk.

• **The Relevant Church.** New communities of faith are popping up around the world and are challenging the traditional church model. *The Relevant Church* shares individual ideas and stories of churches that are engaging a new generation with passionate worship and a life-changing message, all while they impact their communities and change their world. £9.99 from www.equippingthechurch.co.uk.

• **Church, Community and Change** is a Tearfund resource and training programme that enables churches to respond to the needs of their communities in a way that shows God's love and brings about real, lasting and positive change. For a free introductory booklet with more detail please email enquiry@tearfund.org or call 0845 355 8355. When you sign up for the programme you are assigned a facilitator to help you run the course at your church.

• **Compassionate Community Work,** Dave Andrews. This book offers an introductory course on Christlike community work that can be used in both formal and informal settings. £15 from www.micahnetwork.org.

Tools to help you engage and research your community

• **Shaftesbury's** *Information Triangle* explains the points in this chapter in more detail. You can download more information on Shaftesbury's *Information Triangle* at www.shaftesburysociety.org.

• **Shaftesbury's** *Questionnaire Pack* will thoroughly equip you to carry out a community survey and Faithworks also have available a *Community Audit Pack* which contains excellent advice to carry out an audit of your community.

Shaftesbury's Community Mission team:
Jill Clark – Community Mission Co-ordinator.
Tel: 0845 330 6033
Email: communityinfo@shaftesburysociety.org

How can the Bible be made relevant in an urban context?

Web: www.shaftesburysociety.org/ communitymission
Faithworks:
Tel: 020 7450 9031
Email: info@faithworks.info
Web: www.faithworks.info

Training

Faithworks run training courses that can be delivered as one day or half day workshops in your area to help your church develop its role within the local community. It covers four practical modules on turning your vision into reality, being distinctly Christian, grant applications and business planning plus working in partnership with others. Find out more at www.faithworks.info or by emailing info@faithworks.info.

Shaftesbury run bi-monthly training courses in both London and Bradford on issues relating to Christian social action and community development. Some are very practical like how to manage volunteers or deal with conflict and some are theological and ask questions like 'How can the Bible be made relevant in an urban context?' Most of the days are free. Find out more at www. shaftesburysociety.org/communitymission or by emailing jclark@shaftesburysociety.org.

CHAPTER 18
PLANNING THE YEAR

Steve Clifford (Pioneer Inspire / Soul Survivor),
Ian Chisnall (HOPE 08 Co-ordinator)

HOPE will be expressed in amazingly varied ways, from large-scale citywide events with hundreds of churches working together, through to small local village, street or neighbourhood initiatives, developed around a household or small group. Whatever the scale of your involvement, planning really helps. So here are a few suggestions to help you consider working with other churches, linking up with the police, government bodies and other agencies, plus how you can research the needs in your community and your church's ability to meet their needs.

WORKING TOGETHER

For many, involvement in HOPE will come as a church or group of churches in an area committed to working together through 2008. Already numerous forums exist, as leaders of churches, youth groups or organisations in a community get together for encouragement, support and prayer. Examples are local fraternal groups and Church Together groups. These settings have already become wonderful catalysts for planning together for 2008.

Collaboration is one of the key values of HOPE and we have been so encouraged in the planning

'We do it better when we do it together'

stage of HOPE by the support of all the major denominations, networks and bodies such as Churches Together and the Evangelical Alliance. 'We do it better when we do it together', but collaboration will look very different in HOPE initiatives around the country.

- **Joint action (among churches)**
  This could, in some settings, involve a group of churches pooling resources, praying together and planning a year of activities, focused on their communities. Such a level of working together will demand:

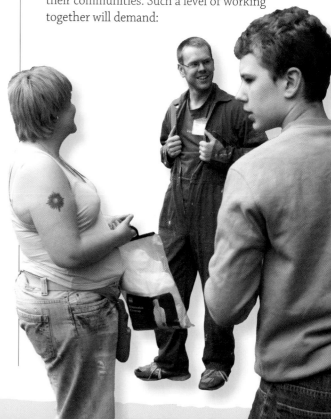

- Leadership.
- Good communication.
- Agreement on decision-making, finances and follow-through.

- **Co-ordinated action (among churches)**

In other settings, a group of churches across an area might agree that while joint action would be appropriate for certain activities, other aspects of the HOPE year would be expressed within the local churches but in a co-ordinated way, so that we agree to profile and support each others' activities and events and thus avoid any sense of competition.

- **Working with Christian agencies (church to agency)**

One of the wonderful discoveries as the HOPE vision began to emerge, was the commitment of Christian agencies (ministries, organisations, denominations, networks) to get behind and make themselves, their expertise, resources, training and personnel available to support HOPE and particularly to be available to churches however large or small to make HOPE happen.

Throughout this publication, numerous references are made to these agencies and the final section endeavours to pull together a directory of resources – providing easy access via a visit to their website – emailing, writing or phoning or accessing publications or training courses.

Most (if not all) of these agencies exist to serve the body of Christ in its mission, so let's make the most of all they have to offer.

- **Working with public bodies**

Please see Chapter 16 for more information on working with the police and government.

RESEARCH

HOPE is about 'transformation' as local churches engage with their communities through words and actions. Such engagement must have integrity. In Chapter 17 we have been challenged to think long-term and strategically.

> Collaboration is one of the key values of HOPE, but collaboration will look very different in initiatives around the country.

> The final section endeavours to pull together a directory of resources.

Strategic planning will involve us asking some key questions, both about ourselves and about the communities we are committed to.

- **About ourselves**

- Who are we? (Age, social and ethnic background, theological persuasion)
- How available are we?
- What resources do we have? (Skills, buildings, finances, personnel)
- What are we already doing? (Is it going well? Could we improve? Are there key relationships in the community which are important to us?)
- Has God been speaking to us?

- **What about our communities?**

Sadly, we often think we know our communities better than we really do! So why not consider a community audit to get an update and assessment of the nature and needs of our communities?

A number of Christian agencies have been working together to produce an effective, yet easy to use, resource enabling us to better understand the nature of our communities. You can download a resource called *Getting to Know Your Neighbours* from the Shaftesbury Society at www.shafetesburysociety.org which tells you everything you need to know about planning and carrying out a community audit. Another way to understand what the issues are in your community is to hold a Poverty Hearing which allows you to hear, from the people you are looking to work with, exactly what their needs are.

Poverty and Homelessness Action Week takes place from 28 January to 3 February 2008 to encourage churches to find out the needs in their community and think about how they can respond. Run jointly by Housing Justice and Church Action on Poverty you can check out their websites at www.housingjustice.org.uk and www.church-poverty.org.uk. For more detail on training for Poverty and Homelessness Action Week contact the HOPE 08 office on 01273 571939 or email info@hope08.com.

What is a Poverty Hearing?

The main purpose of a Poverty Hearing is to provide the opportunity for people with direct experience of poverty to speak out for themselves while encouraging those with power, authority and different experiences to listen. It can take any number of dimensions from a day-long conference, to a series of events, a less formal private forum, an evening meeting or a round table discussion. **The most important thing is that you ensure respect and dignity for people who may feel vulnerable.**

The aim of the Hearing is to empower not to patronise.

A Cautionary Note:
- *Be patient...* **Planning a Poverty Hearing cannot and should not be rushed. Building trust and understanding takes time and must be led by the needs and interests of those who often feel rejected by the wider community.**
- *Be careful...* **As someone who is active in your church or community, you may take for granted those things which remain for others, a daunting challenge: speaking in public, meeting deadlines, organising others to do things, or writing letters.**
- *Be sensitive...* **Personal experience of poverty can leave people feeling extremely vulnerable, but also very proud. The aim of the Hearing is to empower not to patronise; partnerships and friendships can only thrive in an atmosphere in which people feel valued.**

For more details about a Poverty Hearing, download the Church Action on Poverty PDF document *free* from the HOPE website www.hope08.com. This gives you all the information you need from the planning stages, organising the practicalities of the event, through to publicity and post-event follow up.

COMMUNICATING THE HOPE VISION

In order for HOPE to reach its potential, hundreds of thousands of Christians across the UK from all traditions and backgrounds, young and old, need to capture the vision of what HOPE is about and be given an opportunity to make a contribution. What is going to happen at a grassroots level is down to you, but we can help in supporting your communication and vision.

- ***HOPE: Great Ideas for HOPE 08*** – this publication is designed to make HOPE accessible to every small group and church right across the country. If you would like to buy more so that you can give them to key influencers and leaders in your church please visit www.hope08.com or www.authenticmedia.co.uk where you will find details of bulk buy discounts.

- **How to explain HOPE 08.** When producing materials or explaining HOPE 08 you may find it useful to use the following:
HOPE 08 is committed to encouraging churches and organisations of all Christian denominations to get involved in their communities all over the UK and to be the good news of Jesus in both word and deed. HOPE 08 is not prescriptive but provides resources that allow for flexibility so the whole church can reach the whole nation for a whole year and beyond.

- **HOPE DVD.** Available from the HOPE office (email: info@hope08.com) featuring a short HOPE promo suitable for showing at church services or small groups together with a series of practical sections designed to support the planning of HOPE.

- **HOPE literature.** Tells something of the HOPE story and vision and encourages participation. Why not get a supply and make it available both for your own church and for those around you? (Available at no cost from the HOPE office, email details as above).

- **HOPE website.** A one-stop shop for HOPE information which is regularly updated with latest news and fresh resources. Visit www.hope08.com regularly to see what's new.

• **HOPE e-news.** If you register on the HOPE website as a HOPE partner we will send you a regular HOPE e-news update, giving loads of stories, fresh resources and requests for prayer. This information will enable you to keep yourself and others updated on what is happening, not just in your area but right across the country.

Note: Chapter 16 provides you with some resources for communicating what is happening during the HOPE year not only to your church but also to the local newspapers, radio and TV.

USING THE HOPE BRAND

The HOPE brand has been developed as a key resource to provide cohesion to the numerous expressions of HOPE around the country and enable identification with the HOPE vision and values. As such the logo can be freely downloaded from the HOPE website www.hope08.com.

In using the HOPE brand, our simple request is that it should only be used in association with activities which reflect the vision and values of HOPE (please refer to Chapter 1 and the website: www.hope08.com for more details). The HOPE brand has been designed with the flexibility to sit alongside existing brands as a Kitemark, adding to rather than distracting from existing initiatives. In other settings however, the HOPE brand will provide a focal point for activities and as such you are free to use and develop materials which carry the logo. (The HOPE leadership team are grateful for the generosity of ABA-design – website: www. aba-design.co.uk – for their support in donating the HOPE brand. We are thrilled with their work.)

A WHOLE YEAR!

There is no individual, group or church that could possibly take on every 'Great idea' in this book! As the vision for 2008 began to emerge it became clear that HOPE would look very different as one visited villages, towns and cities across the country; flexibility is the order of the day. Why not think of this book as an impressive a la carte menu? Your job is to design a meal (with however many courses you want) that is most appropriate in your particular setting.

There is no individual, group or church that could possibly take on every 'Great idea' in this book!

Chapters 4–15 of this guide contain our ideas. (You might have others. If so, let us know and we will get them on the website.) Just a few comments on the year:

• **Chapter 4 to Chapter 8** follows the church calendar and offers five high points through the year with some wonderfully creative ideas and resources to support engagement with our communities.

• **Chapter 9 and Chapter 10** pick up on the HOPE vision to enable young people to engage effectively in HOPE and be involved in the leadership of many HOPE 08 activities. Wouldn't it be wonderful if HOPE left a legacy of a dynamic 'Youth Movement' motivated to reach their communities with the good news?

• **While some churches tend to spend the summer away,** for others it is a major opportunity for mission. Chapter 11 picks up on some great ideas for the summer of 2008 as Christian agencies such as Urban Saints and YFC rise to the challenge of supporting churches in festivals, fun days, kids clubs, arts and music academies and the like.

• **Chapter 12** gives you some ideas for how to keep engaged with God in prayer before, during and after 2008 both individually and corporately.

• **Chapter 13** offers resources for churches working together across a town or city to engage in large scale co-ordinated activities, using material already field tested by Bible Society and now adapted and made available to us all.

• **Chapter 14 and 15** bring HOPE down to a small group or an individual household level and offers opportunities to engage with your street, neighbourhood or workplace.

Saltmine Theatre Company

Touring ground-breaking, full-scale theatrical productions

Saltmine

Red Balloon Theatre Company

Breathing New Life into Children's Theatre

ReDefined

Hip Hop Performance Duo

CHAPTER 19
PREPARING YOUR CHURCH FOR HOPE

Philip Jinadu (iCQ)

To make the most of the opportunities that HOPE 08 represents, it's absolutely vital that we prepare ourselves and our churches effectively. With proper preparation it is possible to achieve a lasting impact from our mission and social engagement.

The problem is, though, there are different ways to approach this process of preparation and some are more effective than others. So how do we know what approach to take? How do we prepare our churches for outreach in general, and HOPE 08 in particular?

THE KETTLE AND THE SAUCEPAN

When you want to boil water, you can either flick a switch on a kettle or boil a pan of water. Do the first and results are quick; your water will be ready just two noisy minutes later, but it also cools pretty quickly too as the kettle turns itself off. A saucepan takes longer but once the water has boiled it can be kept at the same temperature just by continuing to apply the same heat.

Our models for outreach can look similar. We're tempted to go for a big event, a special initiative to jolt our churches into action. They have a high impact and deliver almost instant results but things quickly settle back to how they were before the event as the action is only short term. Sadly, recent UK church history has plenty of examples of big, dramatic initiatives that were great while

We may use special programmes and initiatives, but they fit within a context of an ongoing culture, and so they help deliver a much more long-term, transforming effect.

they lasted, but had disappointing results in the long term. We don't want HOPE 08 to be like that. Our events should be like the saucepan approach, perhaps less dramatic but much more sustainable over the long term. We need to think about the cumulative, long-term effect of small, sustainable changes, all consistent with an over-arching vision. We may use special programmes and initiatives, but they fit within a context of an ongoing culture, and so they help deliver a much more long-term, transforming effect.

LEADERSHIP, GIFTS AND MOBILISATION

There are three basic areas that we need to focus our preparation efforts on: leadership, gifts and mobilisation.

1. Leadership

The only way HOPE 08 will succeed in a church is if those in leadership take hold of it and lead from the front. As leaders we need to ask ourselves some questions.

The first question is obvious: what is the destination that we want HOPE 08 to take us to? What are we looking to achieve, what impact do we want to have, what are our desired outcomes?

The second question though is much easier to miss: where are we starting from? Unless we have a clear and accurate understanding of the position our church is in right now, we won't know the direction to go in order to reach our goal.

- **What are the main access points** into church life for those that we are reaching? Are they open and clear?
- **Have we thought through** our discipleship process for new believers?
- **How strong** is our outreach culture?
- **How well are we balancing** maintenance and mission? Is mission intrinsically driven from our values or simply a bolt-on to church life?
- **Is our approach to outreach** joined up and strategic?

We need champions of HOPE 08 at the grass-roots level of church life – scattered throughout small groups, ministry teams and community outreach projects.

- **Do we have the right structures** in place for growth and for effective engagement with our communities?
- **Do all our volunteer helpers** have a clear understanding of the vision?
- **Is our overall church health** conducive to church growth?

It's a great idea to do a church audit to see where you are at either by bringing in a church consultant to help your team think through the issues (see Resources section for more information), by scheduling a leadership retreat, by using appropriate books or guides or you could even work through an online church health audit. See Resources for more details.

2. Gifts

We want to make sure the projects and programmes serve the people and that they are empowered to get on board. As we discover what people's gifts are, we empower them to fully use those gifts and fulfil their own God-given vision.

Any lasting change in a church requires catalysts and prime-movers to make it happen at grassroots. We need champions of HOPE 08 at the grass-roots level of church life – scattered throughout small groups, ministry teams and community outreach projects. The more we can encourage, resource and develop those

gifted and motivated for outreach, the bigger the knock-on effect for the rest of church life.

As part of your preparation for HOPE 08, it's worth considering how to develop and utilise the gifts of people already in your church.

- **Who are the potential influencers** in your church?
- **Who are the catalysts,** the cheerleaders for outreach and how can you mobilise them?
- **How can you develop them** and empower them to do what they are already motivated for?
- **How can you help them** expand their influence and increase their leadership capability?
- **What resources** can you put in their hands?
- **What roles and responsibilities** can you trust them with?

Identify and invest in key people with gifts and motivation for outreach to see your potential workforce multiplying dramatically.

3. Mobilisation

The model Jesus gave us was to be incarnational and to get involved with people, which ultimately depends on mobilising every believer to become a missionary.

HOPE 08 gives us a good context to 'up our game' in terms of training for outreach, and provides a natural opportunity for bringing teaching and training to our congregations. It's important that we equip not only for individual witness, but also for corporate outreach. The thrust of so much New Testament growth came from the attraction of a visible community of believers that acted as a 'light on a stand'. In Acts we see a description of the life of the church that was so attractive that people were added daily. After all, Jesus said that it was by our love for one another that people would recognise us as genuine disciples. The best training programmes take this into account.

So the last element of our preparation strategy is to make sure that each member has confidence in the good news message and knows how to communicate it simply and naturally. We've found

> The model Jesus gave us was to be incarnational and to get involved with people, which ultimately depends on mobilising every believer to become a missionary.

lots of great courses and put them in the Resources section so you can find what works for your church to make outreach a natural and sustainable part of your church life.

JUST THE START

It's our prayer that HOPE 08 acts as an invaluable boost to your work in reaching your community, but it will always be most effective as part of an ongoing process. The saucepan should be kept simmering not only before HOPE 08 but during it and long after it.

As you think through your preparation strategy for HOPE and the process beyond that, it's worth bearing in mind this truth: most churches overestimate what they can accomplish in one year, but they *underestimate* what they can accomplish in ten years, or 20 years. We have to think long-term and look to bring hope to our communities for many years to come

RESOURCES

To help your church prepare for HOPE...

Leadership and church auditing

Books
Winning Ways – How to create a culture of outreach in your church, Philip Jinadu and David Lawrence. In this unique and challenging book a pastor and an evangelist

A sample plan

Here's a simple timetable that you could use as a starting point for your planning process.

Sept 07	• Schedule time with the leadership team for a church audit and health check which includes time to talk and pray and to come up with two or three key areas for change and development. • Examine and select training and development resources that will be appropriate for your church.
Oct 07	• Construct a strategic plan for HOPE 08 and beyond with resources available, training needed, prayer plans, publicity and follow up. • Identify and approach key influencers and leaders who can be developed as grassroots leaders for HOPE 08.
Nov 07	• Provide simple training for key leaders to impart vision and ownership, in-house or combined with local churches. • Increase communication of the HOPE 08 vision to the church and schedule some significant prayer initiatives.
Dec 07	• Allocate specific areas of responsibility to grassroots leaders. • Use Christmas to act as a 'dry run' for HOPE 08. Evaluate your strengths and weaknesses accordingly.
Jan to March 08	• Aim for a meeting a month to continue training leaders. • Launch an evangelism training course in small groups to coincide with the launch of HOPE 08 outreach initiatives. • Encourage people to take part in HOPE 08 prayer triplets.
Apr to Dec 08	• Consider supplemental training for church members with sessions on 'Dealing with Difficult Questions', 'Nurturing New Believers', 'Sustaining Outreach Long Term' etc. • Schedule regular leadership times to evaluate the effectiveness of what you're doing. Take on feedback from the congregation and the community at large.

combine forces to point a new way forward. *Winning Ways* provides a fresh model of 'evangelistic leadership' that is both biblical and tested, drawing on material developed and shaped in real-life church situations over a number of years. This is a book for leaders and congregations alike who have a heart for mission, and who long for an approach to outreach that is organic, empowering and, above all, effective. Published by Authentic Media. £8.99 from www.authenticmedia.co.uk.

Online audits

The 'Winning Ways Leaders Consultation'

is an online church health and outreach audit. Using a combination of presentation and guided discussion questions on the issues of discipleship, community and outreach, the consultation provides leaders with a personalised and graphical picture of church health and strategy, with recommendations for development. Available at www.winningwaysweb.com.

Developing gifts

• **Church Growth Academy.** This is an 18-month to two-year process for developing people with a motivation for outreach. It helps produce grassroots evangelistic leaders, and can be started before HOPE, or during HOPE. It uses DVD teaching, personal development goals, resources for church life and access to an online community for models of good practice, discussion and help. For more information and a special HOPE 08 package, please visit www.winningwaysweb.com.

Church consultants

• **If your church is part of a denomination,** then chances are good that there will be some regional ministries set aside to provide an outside perspective for local churches. They may not use the 'consultant' terminology, but look for evangelism advisers, regional superintendents, area team and the like.

It's our prayer that HOPE 08 acts as an invaluable boost to your work in reaching your community.

Music has always been a vital part of church life and now not only helps us express our worship but shapes people's thinking and theology too.

• **Para-church organisations** sometimes provide specific church health and strategy audits for churches. Try contacting those in your local area.

• **Alternatively, consult** the *UK Christian Handbook* for a list of independent, freelance church consultants. (Available from Christian bookshops.)

Outward-focused music

Music has always been a vital part of church life and now not only helps us express our worship but shapes people's thinking and theology too. Much of our music over the last 20 years has emphasised our relationship with God and rightly gives honour and worship to him. But now we face the challenge of adding to that and worshipping God by reflecting our responsibility to be mission-focused.

Ben Wong, a Chinese church leader, said, 'If you want your church to be truly outward focused you ought to consider one in four songs having that kind of dynamic to it.' Until recently that would have been very difficult to do, but many Christian songwriters over the last few years have started to produce music that focuses on God's heart for the world around us and our response to that. The HOPE 08 website will provide up-to-date details of outward-focused music and we hope to be able to provide a CD soon. See www.hope08.com for more details.

• **RUN – Reaching Unchurched Network**
is a growing network of churches passionate about mission in contemporary culture. Members of RUN have access to leading edge outreach thinking and up to date ideas, high quality resources and links with churches and ministries across the UK and beyond to benefit from a wide range of experience. Find out more and join RUN (annual subscription £44 for churches or individuals) at www.run.org.uk

'Imagine – how we can reach the UK', DVD presented by Mark Greene, £10. A 50-minute film about integrating faith with the whole of life, helping your church have a bigger impact and living well as fruitful missionaries – www.licc.org.uk/bookshop.

Evangelistic training initiatives

• *Blowing your Cover* by Kevin Higham and Mike Sprenger. This six-part training course on lifestyle evangelism covers communicating the gospel, connecting with your culture and living a Spirit-filled life. Many resources are available to help you run the course including a *Leader's Guide* (£30), a media DVD pack (£45), a *Blowing Your Cover Workbook* (£7 for one, £30 for a pack of five) and a church resource pack which contains everything you would need to run the course for 15 people (£140, saving £25 on buying individually). For more information and a free sampler DVD see www.blowingyourcover.com.

• **CaFE.** Catholic Faith Exploration (CaFE) run a series called *Pass It On* to help church groups consider their role as evangelists and learn how to run outreach programmes. The course consists of five talks (four x 20 minutes and one x 40 minutes) available on video or audio, a course manual which includes small group discussion questions and a *Pass It On* book taking a more comprehensive look at evangelism. For more details and to order see www.faithcafe.org.

• **DNA.** Part of the Pioneer Trust, DNA is full-time programme running yearly from October–August training you in culturally relevant evangelism and church-based discipleship. You must be at least eighteen years old to take part in DNA but there is no upper age limit. You can find out more and apply online at www.dna-uk.org.

• *Genetik – The Message Trust.* The Tribe Academy is based at the Message Trust and aims to train and equip eighteen to twenty five-year-old evangelists in creative arts and urban mission. In 2008, the Message Trust are raising their game and attempting to deliver HOPE schools missions linked into local churches right across Greater Manchester and huge community action weekends in all ten boroughs. In order to be right at the heart of the action, The Message is offering a special year out. Six months training and equipping as part of the Genetik programme followed by six months hands-on as part of a HOPE 08 team in the schools and estates across the region running from September 2007 to August 2008, or January 2008 to December 2008. For more information contact Genetik@message.org.uk – www.message.org.uk.

• *J John and the Philo Trust. Breaking News* is a six-week evangelistic training book that can be used by individuals, small groups and whole churches. The sessions provide you with

Whatever your church or organisation does as part of Hope 08, don't let your efforts go to waste!

ON ANY MATERIALS YOU PRODUCE:

- be clear about who you are and how people can contact you;
- make it easy for people to find out more about the Christian faith by also including contact details for the Christian Enquiry Agency.

We will send enquirers contemporary materials that introduce them to the life and teaching of Jesus and what it means to follow him today.

We offer follow-up services and support to ensure enquirers can take a next step of faith when ready.

So publicise our contact details alongside yours.

It will cost you nothing and the result could be priceless.

Christian
Enquiry Agency

This is all you need to add to your literature (we do the rest):

To request a free information pack, simply:
- text "HOPE" to 81025
- write to FREEPOST MORE HOPE
- email hope@morehope.info

This service is brought to you by the Christian Enquiry Agency in partnership with (your church name here).

For more details of how we can help you bring hope to your community, call Gareth on 020 8144 7177 or visit:

Charity number 297393

An agency of Churches Together in Britain and Ireland.

www.christianity.org.uk/hope

a readymade training programme to engage you and your church in evangelism. Individual copies are £4.99 but prices are reduced for bulk orders. Please see www.philotrust.com or call 01923 287777.

• **Lost for Words.** *Lost for Words* is a resource to help people of every age share their faith naturally. It includes three separate courses (children, youth and adults) with leader's notes, a CD Rom with PowerPoint presentations, handouts, activities and publicity material. Available from CPAS for £39.95, tel: 01926 458458.

• **Urban Saints in conjunction with Church Pastoral Aid Society and London School of Theology.** *Christian Life and Children* is a series of six sessions on video to teach about

Training you in culturally relevant evangelism and church-based discipleship.

evangelism with children. Each session has three sections to be followed by discussion, Bible study and prayer and the course covers topics including how children grow spiritually, how to build healthier families inside and outside the church, and developing a strategy for effective children's work. Package including video, notes and CD Rom costs £20. See www.urbansaints.org for more details.

• **YFC – The Art of Connecting.** This Youth for Christ course looks at evangelism from the point of view of three stories: yours, your friends and God's. Over the seven weeks, it helps you to see the value of your own testimony and experiences, to listen better to others and to work out how to tell God's story.

Leader's pack (£29 plus £3 p&p) includes leader's guide with activities, discussion starters and interactive teaching, a video and CD to motivate young people to share their story, *The Art of Connecting* paperback book, and a set of cards to be given out upon completion of the course. See www.theartofconnecting.org or www.yfc.co.uk for more detail.

• **YWAM.** Youth With A Mission run a School of Evangelism course that includes looking at character, understanding the good news, and how to effectively communicate it. The course consists of 13 weeks' study followed by a 12-month outreach programme. See www.ywam-england.com for more details.

• **Evangelism Explosion** run a number of courses for both church leaders and congregation members. See www.ee-gb.org.uk for more details.

Books for evangelism

• *Just walk across the room,* Bill Hybels. Simple steps pointing people to faith. Zondervan £6.99. From Christian bookshops.

• *Sharing Jesus in a new millennium,* Rob Frost. Distilling the wisdom gained from 15 years of experience, Rob Frost examines the place of evangelism in contemporary society and sets out the biblical base for mission. Included are hot tips on the kinds of outreach that really work. £5, available from www.sharejesusinternational.com.

• **Sharing the Feast,** Anna Robbins. 'Recipes for evangelism and discipleship for today's church'. Available at £7.99 from store. www.springharvest.org.

• **Becoming a Contagious Christian,** Bill Hybels and Mark Mittelberg and *Building a Contagious Church*, Mark Mittelberg – A range of Zondervan books and DVDs are available on these titles.

• **You're an angel: Being yourself and sharing your faith,** Peter Neilson. This book aims to encourage and reassure all Christians that they can share their faith without fear. Published by Covenanters - £11.95 from www.amazon.co.uk.

• **Beyond the Fringe – Reaching people outside the church,** Nick Pollard. Published by Inter-Varsity Press. £5.99.

• **Telling the Story,** Luis Palau and Timothy L. Robnett. If you've ever wondered 'Have I been called to be an evangelist?' and 'Where do I begin?' this book is for you. A valuable resource for anyone contemplating the call to evangelism, this book includes an extensive appendix with spiritual gifts inventories, directories of evangelistic networks, and checklists for the growing ministry. £10.49 from www.equippingthechurch.co.uk.

• **Dare 2 Share – A Field Guide to Sharing Your Faith,** Greig Stier. This practical handbook focuses on conversation starters, compliments, common ground and the skill of listening, plus helps readers identify their natural style of evangelism and shows you how to defend your faith without offending others. £10.99 from www.equippingthechurch.co.uk.

• **Permission Evangelism,** Michael Simpson. Evangelism without the fear! This book uses proven business and marketing techniques

to encourage evangelism. £7.99 from www.equippingthechurch.co.uk.

• **50 Ways to Share Your Faith,** Ian Knox. Christians know that people need Jesus but often panic at the thought of sharing their faith. Ian Knox has been an evangelist for many years and here shares his mistakes with us as well as his successes in the hope that we will be encouraged in our evangelistic efforts and ultimately know the joy of leading someone to Christ. £8.99 from www.equippingthechurch.co.uk.

• **The Evangelist's Notebook,** John Peters. John looks at what it takes to be an evangelist and shares his own experiences, urging us to concentrate on the essential truths in our evangelism and to be open to the Spirit's leading in our conversations with unbelievers. Published by Kingsway. £8.99 from www.equippingthechurch.co.uk.

• **Ambiguous Evangelism,** Bob Mayo with Sylvie Collins and Sara Savage. In this practical and encouraging book, Bob Mayo helps us to examine evangelism in a culture where people know very little about the Christian faith. £9.99 from www.spck.org.uk.

• **Reaching Single Adults: An Essential Guide for Ministry,** Dennis Franck. A comprehensive handbook to help your church reach the 44 per

cent of adults who are unmarried. £9.99 from www.eden.co.uk.

• **40 Days of Community,** Rick Warren. The latest in The Purpose Driven Life series, this book helps churches deepen authentic community within their church family and reach out to the local community outside the church. Find out more at www.purposedriven.co.uk.

FURTHER RESOURCES FOR EVANGELISM

• **You can download** a free ten-page PDF file on evangelism from the Christians in Sport website www.christiansinsport.org.uk.

• *The Godman* is a 3D animation film that presents the gospel story of Jesus as the Saviour in a way that is accessible to children. You can purchase 'The Godman Mission Pack' for £49.99 which includes the DVD, promotional materials for your church and 200 copies of the *Children's Animated Edition of the Book of Hope* to complement the film. Find out more at www.bookofhope.co.uk and order at www.UCB2GO.co.uk.

• **'In motion'** is an 80-minute DVD designed for use within church services, small groups and outreach events which explores the themes of forgiveness, success, relationships and spirituality to provoke a response to the Christian message. £20 (incl. p&p) from www.run.org.uk.

Christians know that people need Jesus but often panic at the thought of sharing their faith.

• *Game of Life* – An evangelistic resource from J John expressing the Christian message through sport. Single copy £1.99, bulk buy from 45p from www.philotrust.com.

• **UCB's** *Looking for God?* initiative takes people through a unique, internet-based presentation of the gospel, gives them an opportunity to respond and provides practical, personal support to anyone making a decision to accept Christ. See www.lookingforGod.com.

• **THE4POINTS** is a simple but effective way of communicating the gospel with people regardless of age or background. Resources with the 4points symbols include T-shirts, wristbands, balloons, canvas banners, car stickers and badges. Find out more and purchase items at www.4points.co.uk.

Publicity and Outreach Materials for

H0PE 2008

CPO is the leading provider of publicity and outreach materials to the Church in the UK.

We are very excited by the HOPE 2008 project and will be supporting this campaign by providing:

- A range of branded publicity materials including – Posters, Banners, Invitations, Folders and more
- Branded resources and merchandise for outreach and evangelism

Visit our website www.cpo.org.uk/hope08

Sign up to our HOPE 2008 e-newsletter by emailing us your details to
hope08@cpo.org.uk

Christian Publishing & Outreach Ltd
Garcia Estate, Canterbury Road, Worthing, West Sussex BN13 1BW
Tel: 01903 263354 **Fax:** 01903 830066 **E-mail:** sales@cpo.org.uk **Web:** www.cpo.org.uk

resources
& acknowledgements

"Get others involved, share ideas, pool resources and do everything in his name."

CHAPTER 20
RESOURCES DIRECTORY

Chapter 3 / Why bother?

- **Sowing Reaping Keeping**, *Laurence Singlehurst*. This book helps the reader explore what it means to love people, to sow seeds of faith, to reap the harvest at the right time and to nurture growing faith. Published by Inter-Varsity Press. £6.99 from www.ivpbooks.com.

- **Worship Evangelism Justice**, *Mike Pilavachi with Liza Hoeksma*. This book explores the meaning of loving God with all our hearts and loving our neighbours as ourselves, providing practical tips for evangelism and social justice. Published by Survivor. £5.99 from shop.soulsurvivor.com.

- **Intelligent Church: A Journey towards Christ-centered Community**, *Steve Chalke and Anthony Watkis*. This book seeks to reclaim the true heartbeat of the church; the passion to save not itself but the world. Rooted in deep theology but highly practical this book gives you vision of a church that equips its members for frontline work. Published by Zondervan. £7.99.

- **Freestyle**, *Jo Wells and Andy Frost*. A book about radical discipleship, mission and social justice. Published by Authentic Media. £4.99. Read reviews and order from www.sharejesusinternational.com.

- **Church on the Edge**, *Chris Stoddard and Nick Cuthbert*. Exploring foundational principles of culturally relevant mission, looking at how 22 diverse congregations are making a difference in their own community. A book designed to envision, inspire and encourage anyone who is committed to reaching this generation with the gospel. Published by Authentic Media £8.99 (incl. p&p) from www.run.org.uk.

- **RUN** – (Reaching the Unchurched Network) is a growing network of churches passionate about mission in contemporary culture. Members of RUN have access to leading edge outreach thinking and up to date ideas, high quality resources and links with churches and ministries across the UK and beyond to benefit from a wide range of experience. Find out more and join RUN (annual subscription £44 for churches or individuals) at www.run.org.uk.

Chapter 4 / Fresh HOPE (January)

1. Health and fitness

- **For a healthy cooking class;** you could use Rosemary Conley's *Step By Step Low Fat Cookbook* or check out more health and fitness ideas at www.rosemary-conley.co.uk.

- **Walking is a great way to start exercising;** if you'd like to start a weekend walking club visit www.whi.org.uk to find out about walks in your area plus lots of useful information including training for walk leaders.

- **A sports initiative** could be a great way to get active and to bring new people into the group. You could try Youth for Christ's 'Kick Academy' courses; ten-week programmes teaching the gospel and life skills through football. For more information go to www.yfc.co.uk/kickacademy.

- **To start a weight loss programme** at your church see www.weightwatchers.co.uk/about.

- **Check out the Christians in Sport resources.** They support Christians who *Pray* for their friends, *Play* on and off the sports field in a way that honours God and then look to *Say* something of their faith in Jesus. Find out more and check out the free study guides, talks and other resources at www.christiansinsport.org.uk/downloads/index.htm.

2. Work and vocation

- **'The Heart of Success'** is a DVD and workbook by Rob Parsons which will enable individuals to explore the best way to find that illusive balance between life and work.

Visit Care for the Family at www.careforthefamily.org.uk/hope (for Scotland www.careforthefamily.org.uk/scotland and for Northern Ireland www.careforthefamily.org.uk/ni).

• *Love Work Live Life* – a book by David Oliver about how to discover your work and career as your God-given vocation. Available from Care For the Family, details as above.

3. Family and relationships

• **'21st Century Marriage'** and '21st Century Parents' DVDs. Popular speaker and author Rob Parsons explores the joys and challenges of family life in easy-to-view sections – designed to encourage thought and discussion through accompanying workbooks – from Care for the Family, details as before.

• **Connect 2** – a six-part course for newly married couples that has been used across the UK and abroad, which helps those in the early years of marriage address issues of communication, conflict, expectations and intimacy. It also includes marriage preparation for those seeking to make this lifelong commitment –visit Care for the Family,details as before.

• **Family Time** is a ten-session course on parenting and family life for those with young children. The course covers areas like the impact of marriage on family life, communication, how to handle other things that influence children such as TV, computer games, school friends etc.; family values and discipline. All the material you need to run a course is available in the

Family Time book and you can buy additional resources at www.new-wine.org, by calling 020 8799 3778 or by emailing info@new-wine.org. New Wine also run regular training courses for those wishing to run the course. Five DVD set with leader's guide is £75.

• *Family Ministry Manual:* A practical guide for every church seeking to address the needs of families in their surrounding communities. Written for church leaders by church leaders it addresses the common issues and challenges that leaders might experience as they seek to impact their communities from Care for the Family, details as before.

• **Parentplay** is a fun seven-week parenting course by Rachel Bright and Rachel Murrill which includes small group discussions, followed by a messy-play time with the children. It focuses on the needs of children and is committed to seeing family relationships develop. Its core value is that healthy relationships are key to children's healthy growth and development. This parenting course both encourages and challenges parents and has a large emphasis on play, hence making it a lot of fun. It is accessible to the abilities and needs of all parents with children under five. Available as a book for £19.99 from www.authenticmedia.co.uk.

• **Parentalk Parenting Course** is suitable for all ages including those who are expecting children. The course is split into eight sections of 20-minute videos which are flexible in terms of how much or little you

choose to use. Suitable for expectant parents through to those with teenage children, the videos feature Rob Parsons, Steve Chalke and Dr Caroline Dickinson. Available with a video, leaders guide, activity sheet and magazines to aid completion of the course for £49.95 (plus £2.50 p&p) from www.parentalk.org.uk.

• **Romance Academy** is a sex and relationship education programme (as seen on BBC 2) run specifically for teens that has an excellent format and content that could be ideal for your youth group and their friends. See www.romanceacademy.org for more details.

• **The Marriage Preparation Course** (for engaged couples) and The Marriage Course (for couples who have been married for any length of time) by Holy Trinity Brompton are for any couple that wants to develop or build strong foundations for a healthy marriage that will last a lifetime. Full information and resources for running a course are available from http://themarriagecourse.org and http://themarriagecourse.org/preparation.

• **'The Sixty Minute Marriage'** and 'The Sixty Minute Parent' are available as DVDs and videos with accompanying workbook and books addressing the big questions in marriage and parenthood from www.careforthefamily.org.uk/hope (for Scotland www.careforthefamily.org.uk/scotland and for Northern Ireland www.careforthefamily.org.uk/ni).

• **Marriage God's Way** is a course that can be used by individuals, groups and couples interested in exploring the biblical view of marriage and addressing the biggest challenges relationships face. The pack features two DVDs, audiocassette and one workbook from Selwyn Hughes. £39.95 from www.cwrstore.org.uk.

Further reading
• *The Highway Code for Marriage*, Michael and Hilary Perrott. This best-selling book is for anyone who is about to get married, thinking of giving up on their marriage or wanting to make their marriage even better. £6.99 from www.cwrstore.org.uk.
• *The Highway Code for Parenting*, Michael and Hilary Perrott. This guide for parents deals with the big picture: love and self-esteem, discipline, character development and equipping children for life. It's suitable for Christian and non-Christian alike, and will be welcomed by anyone about to become a parent, feeling overwhelmed, or wanting to enjoy family life more. £6.99 from www.cwrstore.org.uk.
• *Look before you leap* and *Till death us do part* both by J John are two key books about making marriage work. £6.99 each or £9.98 for both. www.philotrust.com
• *Marriage as God Intended*, Selwyn Hughes. Drawing on his many years of experience as a counsellor and husband, Selwyn blends biblical principles with practical suggestions on how to let God keep your marriage at its best. £6.99 from www.cwrstore.org.uk.

4. Financial Freedom
• **The Money Secret Adult Education Course** – designed to provide realistic and grounded advice about finance and debt which will not only improve the lives of many families, but will also proactively reduce relationship, marriage and family break-ups. Available as a book, CD and a workbook from www.careforthefamily.org.uk/hope (for Scotland www.careforthefamily.org.uk/scotland and for Northern Ireland www.careforthefamily.org.uk/ni).
Useful reading: *Your Money and Your Life*, Keith Tondeur. Published by Triangle. An in-depth look at all biblical teaching on money issues and their practical outworking. This is also available as a course looking at money and possessions, budgeting, giving, saving, debt, work and family and ethical considerations. See www.creditaction.org.uk for more details and to download self-help guides, money saving tips and information sheets.

www.moneybasics.co.uk is a useful website produced in partnership with Credit Action, Consumer Credit Counselling Service and GE Money. Contains useful information on handling money and dealing with debt.

5. Kicking It
• **Local secular organisations** may be able to help you find good ways of supporting people; for example try your Primary Care Trust (or Local Health board in Wales) for information about giving up smoking.

Chapter 5 / The Big HOPE (Easter)

Environment
• **For more information** on environmental issues such as climate change see the Campaigning section of www.tearfund.org.

Evangelistic resources to give away

· *Easter SONrise* is an evangelistic resource explaining the truth and significance of Easter as well as outlining the history of many Easter traditions. Price £1.99 single copy, prices reduced for bulk buy – visit www.philotrust.com for more detail and to order.

· *What is a Real Christian?*, Luis Palau. Luis Palau presents the basics of the gospel in straightforward language. He explodes many common myths about what makes a Christian before going on to reveal the truth – and the steps people need to take in order to become children of God. Pack of 6, £4.99, individual copies, 99p. Order from www.cwrstore.org.uk.

Film

· *Reel Issues* – Bible Society monthly magazine that gives you stimulating material to talk about the latest must-see films in the light of the Bible. To subscribe visit www.biblesociety.org.uk – £21 for 12-month subscription (monthly issues are accessed online). For Scottish Bible Society resources see www.scottishbiblesociety.org. For resources from Bible Society in Northern Ireland see www.bsni.co.uk.

· **At www.agape.org.uk/store** you will find a number of versions of the Jesus film including resources for small groups and schools.

· *Passion for the Movies,* J John and Mark Stibbe, £8.99 from www.philotrust.com.

General

· **For Easter resources to use with your youth group**, go to www. lifewords-global.com/easter.

· **www.rejesus.co.uk** have many Easter-themed resources, see their website for more details.

· **'Easter SONrise'** *DVD:* A live-recording of J John speaking at Hillsong London explaining the truth and significance of Easter. £9.99 from www.philotrust.com. Accompanying booklet £1.99 or from 45p if you bulk buy.

· *Easter Cracked* is full of ideas for Easter celebrations, evangelistic outreach for the whole family, craft, drama and events. There are ideas for all-age events for Passover and Good Friday plus assembly outlines and ideas for working with youth and the under five age group. £9.99 from www.scriptureunion.org.uk. For resources from Scripture Union Scotland see www.suscotland.org. uk, for Scripture Union Northern Ireland see www.suni.co.uk.

· *Celebrating the seder,* Nick Fawcett. This book teaches Christians about the Jewish Passover tradition and enables you to hold your own seder meal. With extensive background information, a guide to the Hebrew terms, a section of recipes, a list of useful websites and practical advice and guidance at every stage. £12.99 from www.kevinmayhew.com.

· **CPO** (Christian Publishing & Outreach) produces a wide range of posters, banners, invitation cards, booklets, tracts and other outreach resources specifically themed for

use at Easter and will have specific HOPE 08 resources available from www.cpo.org.uk/hope08. A team of outreach advisors are available on 01903 263354 to help suggest the most appropriate resources for local needs.

Grief

A Grief Observed, C.S. Lewis. Published by Zondervan. £6.99 from www.wesleyowen.com.

When Life is Changed Forever, Rick Taylor, www.careforthefamily. org.uk/hope (for Scotland www.careforthefamily. org.uk/scotland, for Northern Ireland www.careforthefamily.org.uk/ni).

Help my kids are hurting, Marv Penner. Published by Zondervan. £4.99 from www.wesleyowen.com.

Lent

· **Just Church** from Church Action Against Poverty is a course that could be used at Lent which helps churches focus on what they can do practically to engage with social justice and poverty issues around

them. The course is split into ten to 12 modules that can be run over any time period, or sections can be chosen that are of particular interest to the group. Find out more at www.church-poverty.org.uk.

• **Life Source** is a five-session course on prayer for Lent by Robert Warren and Kate Bruce encouraging a discovery of new-found joy and delight in prayer for novices and old hands alike. The course combines Bible study and discussion with a creative, hands-on exploration of five prayer patterns drawn from our rich Christian heritage. £3.99 from www.chpublishing.co.uk.

Passion plays

• **Saltmine** have passion plays that are fast moving and easy to perform. See www.saltmine.org for more details.

Chapter 6 / HOPE on the streets (May Bank Holiday/Pentecost)

• **GO:LOCAL** CD Rom from Soul Action. This CD Rom gives you loads of practical advice about doing Jesus-centred community work. See www.soulaction.org for more detail.

Books

• **Express Community**, by Phil Bowyer, is an inspirational and practical guide to give young people the methods and principles needed for social action. Suitable for youth, student and young adult groups, plus teachers and schools workers this book shows how evangelism and social action are inextricably linked. £7.99 from www.youth.tearfund.org.

• **Everybody Wants to Change the World,** Tony Campolo. More than a hundred practical ideas for compassionately responding to the needs of others. Including suggestions about working with those in poverty, honouring and assisting the elderly; helping immigrants assimilate and supporting the sick; respecting and serving the disabled, showing compassion to those in prison, and caring for the environment. A leader's guide makes this adaptable for group study, as well as individual reading. £10.49 from www.equippingthechurch.co.uk.

• **Building a Better World: Faith at work for change in society**, Malcolm Duncan. This book invites anyone who longs for a fairer world to consider whether commitment to justice could be strengthened by Christian spirituality. £7.99 from www.faithworks.info.

• **What can one person do?** Edited by Sabina Alkire and Edmund Newell. Is the problem of poverty too much for individuals, churches and communities to tackle? This book offers practical suggestions for real things we can do in our personal lives to bring the vision of a world without poverty a step closer. £12.95 from www.dltbooks.com.

General

· See www.soulaction.org for more information on 'Noise' weekends and to download helpful resources such as consent and volunteer application forms.

· Be inspired by the work of Eden, the Message Trust's cutting edge incarnational church planting movement. In the last ten years, 300 Urban Missionaries have moved onto Manchester's toughest estates and right across the region churches are growing and crime is coming down. As part of HOPE 08 The Message would love to help and encourage others to do something similar on their local deprived estates. If you would like help, advice, or resources contact eden@message.org.uk.

· In Wales, GWEINI (the council for the Christian voluntary sector in Wales) provides an umbrella organisation and resources for churches who want to get involved in longer term community projects. See www.gweini.org.uk and the book *The Naked Church* for more detail (published by GWEINI, £6.50 incl. p&p.)

Chapter 7 / HOPE explored (September)

Evangelistic courses and resources

1. Alpha

The Alpha course is a practical introduction to the Christian faith, designed primarily for non-churchgoers and new Christians. Alpha aims to present the core truths of the Christian faith around which Christians of every denomination can unite.

The course is normally run over a period of ten weeks with a weekend or day away halfway through. A typical evening consists of supper, followed by a short time of worship, a talk that can be given live or shown on DVD/VHS and, after the talk, coffee and small-group discussion. Over the ten-week course, 15 topics are addressed such as 'Who is Jesus?' and 'How can we have faith?' and 'Is there more to life than this?'

If you would like to find out more or to come along to be trained on how to run an Alpha course, please see www.alpha.org for details on an Alpha conference or a local Saturday Equip and Refresh training day near you.

Youth Alpha

Youth Alpha is low-key, friendly and fun. It runs on the same basis as Alpha but is tailored to the eleven- to eighteen-year-old age group. See www.youthalpha.org.

Alpha for Students

Based on the Alpha material but aimed at students, the course has taken place on campus, in student houses, in churches, at pubs, in cafés and even in McDonald's! See www.alpha.org/students.

Alpha in the Workplace

Designed to fit into busy working schedules, Alpha in the Workplace sessions tend to be shorter than other Alpha meetings and do not include worship times. They tend to take place in lunch hours or even over breakfast and give opportunity for you to engage in meaningful dialogue with your colleagues. See www.alpha.org/workplace.

(You can also find out about *Alpha in Prisons, Alpha in a Catholic Context, Senior Alpha* and *Alpha for Forces* at www.alpha.org.)

2. Christianity Explored

This ten-week course (with a weekend away part way through) explores who Jesus was, what his aims were and what it means to follow him. It is suitable for those looking to understand more about the Christian faith or as a refresher course for those within the church. You can use the materials provided to do the talks yourself or buy the DVDs to show if you would prefer. Full resources are also available to help you run the course including a leader's manual, study guides and promotional materials.

Find out more and purchase resources at www.christianity explored.com.

3. Y Course

The Y Course has eight sessions that explore life's big issues. Each talk is available on DVD, is introduced by Steve Chalke, then speakers from Joel Edwards to Jeff Lucas explore questions like 'Can anyone really know what God is like?' and 'Who wants to be stuck with a bunch of boring old rules?' The DVD also comes with a CD Rom including a Course Leader's Handbook, Group Leader's Guide and Participant Notes. Other materials such as invitation flyers and videos can also be purchased. *Beyond Belief (Y Course)* by Peter Meadows and Joseph Steinberg is available in paperback for £6.99 from www.authenticmedia.co.uk.

Y Course materials are available from major Christian retail outlets and websites.

4. Emmaus: The Way of Faith

Emmaus is a course designed to welcome people into the Christian faith and life of the church, by teaching the basics of Christianity and developing the discipleship of maturer Christians. It is rooted in Jesus' model of evangelism, nurture and discipleship demonstrated in the story of the Emmaus Road. First it encourages evangelism in the local church and provides practical advice on developing contact with those outside of church. The core material is aimed at enquirers, new Christians and those looking for a refresher course and covers the basics of Christian life. The final stage is about deepening an understanding of Christian living and discipleship.

There is also a Youth Emmaus course for those aged eleven to sixteen.

Find out more and purchase supporting resources for both Emmaus and Youth Emmaus at www.e-mmaus. org.uk.

5. ReJesus

ReJesus is a website that was created for individuals and churches to share information about Jesus with those who don't know much about him. Using a website allows people to discover more about the things that interest them, at their own pace. The site is split into five sections which cover the story of Jesus and some of his most famous followers, how Jesus is alive today and how we can meet him, provides simple suggestions for reflection and prayer, allows people to explore different expressions of

Jesus in art and poetry, plus there is opportunity for online discussion.

Visitors can sign up for a free eight-week course (sent via email) that explores 'Developing Happiness' and there are lots of links that can be emailed to interested friends.
See www.rejesus.co.uk for more details.

6. Lyfe Course (Bible Society)

Lyfe is a course designed to help people encounter the Bible and what it has to say about their everyday lives. Small groups meet together regularly, generally in public places like coffee shops and restaurants. They take a passage of Scripture and then discuss what it tells them about God, how it relates to life today and how they can apply the verses practically. Lyfe is accessible to everyone, even those who aren't Christian, and gives time to read, reflect and respond to God's word. Find out more and download your free welcome pack at www.lyfe.org.uk.

7. NOOMA DVD (Zondervan)

NOOMA is about providing spiritual direction in a way that is accessible to people as and when they need it using the popular format of short films available on DVD. Each film comes with a discussion booklet, and topics covered include the meaning of love, suffering and trusting God. See www. nooma.com for more details. DVDs can be ordered from UK Christian bookshop websites.

8. CaFE

Catholic Faith Exploration is a video-based programme that can be used in churches, schools, colleges and prisons. It is designed to run in four short modules which fit into school terms

and aims to get people excited about their faith, provide an opportunity for good community and empower people to share the good news with those around them. Supporting video materials are available.
See www.faithcafe.org for more details.

9. TEN – J John

TEN is a DVD series exploring the relevance of the Bible message today. Each of the ten 45-minute programmes features vox pops, interviews and J John's compelling explanation for the relevance of a commandment God gave us. The sessions highlight the modern need for these timeless truths, for example using the commandment 'Thou shalt not commit adultery' to discuss how to affair-proof your relationship. The box set comes with a user guide to explain how to make the most of the course and provides pointers for further discussion.

See www.philotrust.com for more details and to order resources (£29.99 for the DVD boxset).

10. Youth For Christ sports teams

YFC has a number of mission teams who are available to come alongside churches and schools to run high-profile, professional courses that provoke thought in young people. The courses aim to develop their physical, moral, spiritual and social values and include a Kick Football team, a Fly Basketball team and a Skate team, all of which provide an educational and challenging experience. See www.yfc. co.uk/teams for more details and to book.

effectively. In 2008 Back to Church Sunday is on 28 September. See www.backtochurch.co.uk for more details and to order resources.

· Christians in Sport provide plenty of talks and documents you can download aimed at people investigating Christianity. See the Investigating Christianity section at www.christiansinsport.org.uk.

· Reel Issues from Bible Society, £21 for 12-month subscription (monthly issues are accessed on line) see www.biblesociety.org.uk. For Scottish Bible Society resources see www.scottishbiblesociety.org. For resources from Bible Society in Northern Ireland see www.bsni.co.uk.

· Passion for the Movies, J John and Mark Stibbe, £8.99 from www.philotrust.com.

11. The Essence Course

The Essence Course aims to provide a way for the church to reach out to those who are currently seeking their own spiritual truth in New Age activities and elsewhere. Held in a neutral environment (e.g. a pub, library or gym) the course runs over a six-week period or as a residential weekend and provides an experiential introduction to the Christian Faith – www.sharejesusinternational.com.

12. Start!

Start! By Robin Gamble is a six-session basic introduction to the Christian faith which assumes no previous knowledge and is often used pre-Alpha. The sessions use a mix of videos, time to chat, discussion activities and time

for reflection in a down to earth way. It is designed to help people think about where they are going in their lives, to discover the good news of Jesus and to decide how they want to respond.

Available from CPAS for £39.95. Tel: 01926 458458, www.cpas.org.uk.

FURTHER RESOURCES

· Back to Church Sunday is a Church of England initiative to provide a warm welcome to anyone who hasn't been to church in a while as well as those who have never been. This can be linked to Harvest or run as a separate event and resources are available (such as T-shirts, prayer cards and posters) to help you advertise the day

Chapter 8 / The Gift of HOPE (Christmas)

Evangelistic resources to give away

• **'More to Christmas'** DVDs from Viz-a-Viz come gift-wrapped and contain stories of 11 people for whom Jesus is making a real difference in their lives. At just £2 a copy this is an affordable and quality evangelistic tool, also available as a magazine for £1. See www.vizaviz.org.uk for more details and to order.

• **More than a Christmas Carol, It's a Wonderful Life** and **What's the point of Christmas?** are all booklets produced by J John's Philo Trust exploring themes

of Christmas using well-known Christmas films and traditions. Single copies £1.99, bulk buy from 45p per copy, www.philotrust.com.

• *God With Us* from Lifewords is a slim publication telling the Christmas story in the Bible's own words suitable to give away at services and events. There is space to write your own message or to add your church details and can be given away as a Christmas card. See www.lifewords.info/christmas.

Events

• **More to Christmas Event:** More to Christmas is a professionally produced, entertaining and thought-provoking multimedia event ideal for Christians and non-Christians. Viz-a-Viz will provide speakers, hosts and a theatre group to perform as well as multimedia material for this two-hour production. An ideal opportunity

to work with other churches in your area to hire a neutral venue such as a school hall or theatre for around five hundred to a thousand people. To find out more and discuss costs, contact Viz-a-Viz via their website www.vizaviz.org.uk/moretochristmasevent.htm or by calling 01268 530531.

General

• **Lifewords:** creative resources for faith-centred living: Lifewords is an international mission agency that exists to connect people with the Bible and to each other – and to experience the relationship with the God that it speaks about. They produce creative, meaningful ways to help people connect to the Bible's life words as an essential part of everyday life and worship as individuals, and as a church.

Their range of booklets, toolkits, and new media resources help tell

the Bible's story and involve others in the conversation. All Lifewords materials are designed for you to use and adapt to connect life words in your own culture, in your own world, in your own way. Order, download, share ideas, and join the conversation at www.lifewords-global.com/uk.

• **CPO (Christian Publishing & Outreach)** produces a wide range of posters, banners, invitation cards, booklets, tracts and other outreach resources specifically themed for use at Christmas and will have specific HOPE 08 resources available from www.cpo.org.uk/hope08. A team of outreach advisors are available on 01903 263354 to help suggest the most appropriate resources for local needs.

• **www.rejesus.co.uk/christmas** have many Christmas specific resources including an overview of the Christmas story, karaoke carols, nativity puzzles, prayers and meditations and a look at the Father Christmas tradition.

• **Youth for Christ** Christmas resources suitable for your youth group are available free from www.hope08.com.

• **Graham Kendrick** is producing an album for Christmas 2008 with the theme of HOPE 08 in mind. Find out more at www.hope08.com.

• **'Christmas Unwrapped'** DVD: A live recording, J John speaking at Hillsong London unpacking the true meaning of Christmas. Aimed at the unchurched but enjoyable for everyone. £9.99 from www.philotrust.com.

HOPE for *New* CHRISTIANS

Every Day with Jesus for New Christians

ISBN-13: 978-1-85345-133-1
ISBN-10: 1-85345-133-9

Inspiring Women Every Day for New Christians

ISBN-13: 978-1-85345-350-2
ISBN-10: 1-85345-350-1

YP's for New Christians

ISBN-13: 978-1-85345-105-8
ISBN-10: 1-85345-105-3

Topz for New Christians

ISBN-13: 978-1-85345-104-1
ISBN-10: 1-85345-104-5

£2.49 each (plus p&p)

Price correct at time of printing

Available from CWR on 01252 784710 or visit our online store at www.cwrstore.org.uk quoting promotion code HR03-210

Also available from your local Christian bookshop

Publications

- **Christmas Wrapped Up** and *Christmas Re-Wrapped* are two publications from Scripture Union that are bursting with ideas for all ages for outreach and celebration at Christmas.
Visit www.scriptureunion.org.uk for more detail and to order. For resources from Scripture Union Scotland see www.suscotland.org.uk, for Scripture Union Northern Ireland see www.suni.co.uk.

- **Together for a Season** – *All-age material for Advent, Christmas and Epiphany,*
Gill Ambrose, Peter Craig-Wild, Diane Craven, Mary Hawes.
A practical resource book full of creative ideas to transform the seasonal liturgy of Advent, Christmas and Epiphany into a multi-sensory and interactive worship experience for all ages. It includes: fully worked out services, step-by-step instructions on ways to introduce creative elements into services and suggestions on how to use the ideas in group work, homes and outreach activities.
£22.50 includes free CD Rom from www.chpublishing.co.uk.

Tackling Poverty

- **Compassion** produces a number of *free* resources to help your church explore their Christian responsibility to those living in poverty. Each resource includes a DVD and Bible study booklet that will help you to get to grips with poverty and how we can make a lasting difference.

1. Hand in Hand. Join Jeff Lucas in Ethiopia to explore how churches are changing lives and shaping futures with the help of Compassion.

2. Bridges of Hope – J John explores how we need to share our faith in word and deed.

3. A Life of Love – Graham Kendrick explains why helping those living in poverty is at the heart of worship.

Find out more about Compassion and order resources free from www.compassionuk.org.

- **Samaritan's Purse:** Sermon outlines, invitations, posters and other ideas for your Shoe Box Sunday, as well as regional contacts and the opportunity to work together with your local Shoe Box community is available on the website: www.samaritanspurse.uk.com. Leaflets on how to pack a shoe box, posters for the campaign, campaign video/DVD can all be ordered from the website as well.

RESOURCES FOR CHILDREN

- **Cool Christmas** is a booklet from J John's Philo Trust helping children aged three to six discover what Christmas is all about. Single copies £1.99, bulk buy from 45p per copy, www.philotrust.com.

- **Christmas Treasures** also by J John is aimed at children aged six to nine exploring the customs and traditions around the festive season. Single copies £1.99, bulk buy from 45p per copy, www.philotrust.com.

Chapter 9 / The HOPE Revolution

Training and Events

- **Soul Survivor** run five-day events aimed at teenagers and one for students and twenty-somethings (called Momentum). Each conference in 2008 will have a seminar stream dedicated to equipping young people for evangelism and mission. Find out more about Soul Survivor at www.soulsurvivor.com/uk (seminar details will be available nearer the time). Dates for 2008: 18-22 July: Momentum, 11-15 August: Soul Survivor Week A, 16-21 August: Soul Survivor Week B.

- **The Art of Connecting** is a seven-week training course from Youth for Christ to help young people to share their faith. It's about realising the value of your own story, God's story and the stories of other people. The course enables young people to adopt great listening skills, go deeper into knowing more of God's story, to see the value of their own and others' stories, and change their relationships for ever. For further information visit www.theartofconnecting.org.

General

- **yfcONE HOPE Teams.** Youth for Christ have been offering opportunities for young people to engage in mission for over 25 years; using the diverse God given skills and abilities young people bring to impact the lives of other young people where it matters most. yfcONE during HOPE 08 are looking for volunteers and locations to enable effective mission to take place; working in prisons, on the streets, in schools, using sport, drama, dance and great youth work to connect with young people. An additional team will be recruited as part of the specialist HOPE teams working in villages, towns and cities near you to make an impact. If you are eighteen to twenty-five and up for the challenge, contact us on www.yfcone.com. Youth for Christ also offer a full mission consultation and delivery package for your area, helping you to deliver mission in a language young people understand.

• **Teenagers in Scotland** can get involved with Fire Starters – a group of Christians who meet together once a month to share God's life and love with one another and with the nation. Fire Starters also provide ongoing leadership training and equipping.
Find out more at www.firestartersuk.org and www.myspace/firestartersforjesus.

• **For young people interested in sport,** Christians in Sport have Bible studies, talks and CDs specifically tailored for them that you can buy or download for free at www.christiansinsport.org.uk/youth_sport/youth_resources.htm.

• **Different denominations employ Youth Officers** – try getting in touch with your local representative and consider who else is working with youth in your area to see if you can work together.

• **Be inspired by 24-7 prayer,** a missionary movement started by young people that has been founded on prayer. Find out more at www.24-7prayer.com.

Publications

• **Xcelerate:** *The evangelist's heartbeat*, Matt Wilson and Andy Hawthorne. This book contains valuable lessons from The Message Evangelism Training School in Manchester connected with the Eden and Tribe projects. £6.99 from www.standrewsbookshop.co.uk.

• **12 Disciples,** Andy Flannagan with Anne Calver. Featuring gritty, unforgettable stories of faith, hope and love that highlight how young people connected to Youth for Christ are being good news. Their stories are aligned with teaching on the story of another disciple who experienced similar ups and downs on his journey – Simon Peter. £7.99 from www.lion-publishing.co.uk.

• **Mission-shaped Youth,** Tim Sudworth, Graham Cray, Chris Russell. Following on from

Mission-shaped Church, this book examines what it means to have a 'youth-mission-shaped church' and challenges us to intersect with today's young people in their daily lives and culture. The authors urge us to offer a mission that isn't just about evangelism, but is also about supporting pastorally and spiritually. £7.99 from www.chpublishing.co.uk.

- **Young People and Mission,** edited by David Brooker. This book grapples with subjects that include helping teenagers to share their faith, ecology and mission, living in a multi-faith society and making the most of a gap year. Challenging, practical, informative and insightful, *Young People and Mission* will help us to re-think the way we do mission with and to young people – inside and outside the church. £8.99 from www.chpublishing.co.uk.

- **The Manga Bible.** The Bible is brought to life in a new way using the dynamic style of Manga comics (the fastest growing genre in British and American publishing). Particularly suitable for teenagers and young adults *The Manga Bible* is a faithful interpretation of the scriptures using beautiful and dramatic artwork. See more details at www.themangabible.co.uk. £8.99 from www.hodderchristianbooks.co.uk.

- **Live the Life,** Mike Pilavachi and Craig Borlase. This funny and accessible book encourages teenagers to follow Jesus in all areas of their life. £7.99 from www.hodderchristianbooks.co.uk.

- **SUbmerge** is designed to encourage eleven to fourteen-year-olds develop a habit of reading their Bible helping them to engage through music, reflection, art and communicating with others. Published every two months (from October 2007) for £2 per copy (subscriptions available). See www.scriptureunion.org.uk for more detail and to order. For resources from Scripture Union Scotland see www.suscotland.org.uk, for Scripture Union Northern Ireland see www.suni.co.uk

Chapter 10 / HOPE in schools and colleges

The HOPE 08 website will provide links to many resources available to buy or download including a students, churches and chaplaincies paper, lesson and assembly materials and lunch club ideas – see www.hope08.com.

- **Support Your Local School:** A guide to opportunities for church involvement in schools. A downloadable PDF file with the nuts and bolts of how you can work in your local schools.

- **Effective Schoolswork:** A book written by experienced schools worker, Lee Jackson. Available as a free download. www.schoolsministrynetwork.co.uk. Includes tips on how to approach schools.

- **You can download resources** for Christian clubs in secondary schools from the Re:source section of the Scripture Union website www.scriptureunion.org.uk. For resources from Scripture Union Scotland see www.suscotland.org.uk, for Scripture Union Northern Ireland see www.suni.co.uk.

- **Sport is a popular and accessible subject** for young people and can be easily linked to Christian values. Get free downloads for youth leaders and teachers, from practical 'how to' fact sheets through to assembly outlines, from www.christiansinsport.org.uk.

- **'Book of Hope'** produce a number of editions aimed at school-age children (five to eight, eight to

eleven, eleven to fourteen and fifteen to twenty), helping children looking at issues like self-esteem, caring for others, peaceful problem solving and understanding their purpose in life. Younger additions include games and exercises while older versions have a magazine style.

There are also accompanying Teacher's Manuals. Find out more and order at www.bookofhope.co.uk.

• **The Youth Emmaus** course is designed to help those aged eleven to sixteen explore the basics of the Christian faith and can be run in schools during lunchtime or as after school study groups. With leader's notes, handouts for group members, great cartoons and graphics and a free CD Rom stacked with other useful resources. £19.95 from www.e-mmaus.org.uk.

• **Jam magazine** contains interviews, articles about films and issues facing teenagers.
Order at www.jammag.co.uk for £1.99.

• **Scripture Union** produces a number of resources suitable for use in schools and with school-age children:

- They hold two five-day residential training courses 'Training in Schools Work' and 'Advanced School for Schools Workers'.

- *So, Why God?*, *Streetwise, Awesome, Rocky Road* and *Bulls Eye* are materials that can be used with school-age children looking to find out more about God, answering questions on why there is suffering, why we pray and who God and Jesus are. £9.99.

- *Into the Bible – 101 routes to explore* is aimed at Keystage 2 children and includes material to equip teachers of all faith backgrounds to use the material with integrity (this could be a good resource for your church to buy your local school).

- 'Top Tips' is a series of booklets which includes the titles *Reaching unchurched children*, *Growing families with faith* and *Welcoming children of other faiths*. £2.99 each or four for £10.

Find out more about these and other training and resources at www.scriptureunion.org.uk (click on Training or Resources). For resources from Scripture Union Scotland see www.suscotland.org.uk, for Scripture Union Northern Ireland see www.suni.co.uk.

• **Assemblies Resource Book** and *Assemblies Resources Through the Year* are full of ideas for fresh and fun assemblies in primary schools covering stories from the Bible and Festivals of World Religions. £10.99 from www.spck.org.uk. You can also access ideas online at www.assemblies.org.uk.

The Big Deal is an initiative that is planning to host a High Schools Mission in the vast majority of Greater Manchester's high schools. Find out more at www.bigdeal.org.uk.

Other useful websites

www.agape.org.uk/students
www.christiansinsport.org.uk
www.cmf.org.uk

www.fairtrade.org.uk/get_involved_university.htm
www.ficu.edu
www.fusion.uk.com
www.loveyouruni.org
www.navigators.co.uk
www.peopleandplanet.org/ftunis
www.relessonsonline.com
www.schoolswork.co.uk
www.speak.org.uk/campaigns
www.alpha.org/students
www.talkingdonkey.co.uk
www.tearfund.org/youth/students
www.uccf.org.uk
www.talkingdonkey.co.uk
www.tearfund.org/youth/students
www.uccf.org.uk

Chapter 11 / HOPE over the summer

• **Want to put on a sporting event?**
Download great fact sheets and 'how to' guides from the Christians in Sport website, including how to run a sports tournament, how to put on a big screen event and how to run a sports holiday club. Visit www.christiansinsport.org.uk

• **MJK** is a ministry that uses a state-of-the-art concert-truck with inbuilt stage, PA and lighting. It uses rappers, DJs and evangelists to get the gospel message across. Open to working alongside churches in a variety of outreach settings, some of which might include fun days, street outreaches and youth events.

Find out more by contacting MJK at www.makejesusknown.com, emailing info@makejesusknown.com or calling 0161 728 1522.

• **Champions Challenge** is a holiday club based on Mark's Gospel with games, drama and craft all around an Olympics theme. Order your pack (available from December 2007) for £9.99 from www.scriptureunion.org.uk. For resources from Scripture Union Scotland see www.suscotland.org.uk, for Scripture Union Northern Ireland see www.suni.co.uk.

• **KidzKlubs** are an excellent way to reach out to communities either as a one-off holiday club or as part of an on-going programme. There are currently hundreds of Kidz Klubs operating across the UK and beyond. For more information on how to run a KidzKlub and resources please visit www.kidzklub.biz.

Chapter 12 / HOPE-filled prayer

Websites

www.24-7prayer.com – Find out more about the 24-7 prayer movement, read about prayer and boiler rooms, as well as checking out other people's prayer stories

www.rejesus.co.uk/spirituality - learn to pray, post a prayer, download a prayer, find a sacred space and learn about prayer labyrinths

www.worldprayer.org.uk for Year of Prayer 2007 Friday Focus themes. Email: prayer@worldprayer.org.uk

www.prayerinaction.net

www.40-days.com – includes a free download of a 40 prayer guide produced by There is Hope

www.pray-as-you-go.org – Pray-as-you-go is a daily prayer session, designed for use on portable MP3 players (or computer), to help you pray while travelling. Free to download

www.radiantlight.org.uk – encouragement in the Catholic faith through paintings and meditations

www.waymakers.org – free monthly email prayer guide helping focus prayer for those not following Jesus Christ

www.noonministries.com – NOON (Need Of Our Nation) encourage people to pray for one hour between noon and one o'clock for our nation

www.schoolsprayernetwork.org.uk – prayer for schools

www.healingrooms.com

www.gg2w.org.uk – Getting God to Work

www.when2pray.net – helping couples pray together

www.crossrhythms.co.uk/prayerrooms – add your own prayers at The Incinerator

www.prayer-alert.net – weekly prayer email for national European and world current issues

Books

Prayer – Unwrapping the gift, John Preston. Encouraging the local church to pray with photocopyable prayer resources, including a prayer audit. Published by Authentic Media. £3.50 from www.authenticmedia.co.uk.

Your Kingdom Come, J John. Study guide for home groups on the Lord's Prayer. £3.50 from www.philotrust.com.

Ignite, Nigel James and Carl Brettle. Seven ways to ignite outrageous prayer, Published by Authentic Media. £7.99 from www.authenticmedia.co.uk.

Grove Booklets Spirituality series such as *Simple Tools for Stillness,* Wanda Nash. Available for £2.95 from www.grovebooks.co.uk.

God 360, Andy Flanagan. 120 experiential devotionals, published by Authentic £8.99 from http://store. springharvest.org.

The 24-7 Prayer Manual and CD Rom, published by Kingsway £9.99, order from www.equippingthechurch.co.uk.

Prayerworks – The Manual, 24-7 and Faithworks, Published by Authentic £6.99 from http://store. springharvest.org.

Community Prayer Cells – How to be good news neighbours, Jane Holloway. Church Pastoral Aid Society. £5 from www.cpas.org.uk.

Pocket Prayers for Work, compiled by Mark Greene. £5.99 from www.chpublishing.co.uk.

Miscellaneous

• **Saints at Prayer,** Michael Mitton. This course is an ideal resource to teach people to pray in groups with confidence. Available from ReSource, 01235 553922 www.resource-arm. net: £7 Leader's Manual, £4 Link Workbook.

• **Prayer Magazine.** A quarterly, interdenominational publication strengthening Christians, churches and prayer groups across Great Britain and Ireland, featuring articles on HOPE 08. Bulk copies for your church or prayer group from 95p a copy, and individual subscriptions from only £9.99 for one year.
To order copies or for further information call 0115 921 7280, email prayer@newlifepublishing.co.uk or visit www.newlifepublishing.co.uk.

• **Purify CD,** Graham Kendrick. A journey of reflection with songs. £3 from www.care.org.uk/shop

• **Ignition cards** help you pray for three friends who aren't Christians. Order free by emailing info@igniteme. org. See www.igniteme.org for more detail.

• **CARE** publish a quarterly prayer diary which will feature HOPE 08 prayer updates – see www.care.org.uk.

Chapter 14 / HOPE and your small group

• **Evangelism Through Cells,** a booklet by Liz West and Laurence Singlehurst, available from Cell UK for £3.50. Tel: 01582 463232.

• **Sowing, Reaping, Keeping,** Laurence Singlehurst. This book helps the reader explore what it means to love people, to sow seeds of faith, to reap the harvest at the right time and to nurture growing faith. Published by Inter-Varsity Press. £6.99 from www.ivpbooks.com.

• **Cell UK** produce a magazine four times a year with inspiring articles and practical ideas for cell leaders. Available via www.celluk.org.uk.

Chapter 15 / Being a good neighbour

• **Sowing, Reaping, Keeping,** Laurence Singlehurst. This book helps the reader explore what it means to love people, to sow seeds of faith, to reap the harvest at the right time and to nurture

growing faith. Published by Inter-Varsity Press. £6.99 from www.ivpbooks.com.

• **Angels on your doorstep,** Paddy Beresford. Published by Kingsway. £6.99 from www.equippingthechurch.co.uk.

• **If you would value support in your workplace,** the opportunity to talk to other Christians about the pressures and problems you face, or just want to feel encouraged in your efforts to bring God's kingdom to your work why not consider joining Bands? These small groups meet in workplaces around the country, offering support and friendship – find out more at www.citybands.co.uk.

• **Being a Christian in the workplace** – www.gg2w.org.uk

• **Community Prayer Cells** – *How to be good news neighbours*, Jane Holloway. Church Pastoral Aid Society. £5 from www.cpas.org.uk.

Chapter 16 / Working with the police, government and the media

• **The Faithworks Local Media Guide** – a beginner's guide designed to help churches and Christian community projects make the most of local media. See www.faithworks.info for more information or email info@faithworks.info.

• **How to be Heard in a Noisy World,** Phil Creighton. Whether it's improving the notice board, maximising the effect of the Sunday experience, or sending the right information to your local paper,

Phil Creighton has the answers. Packed with cost-effective tips and advice, this covers every aspect of church communication and will help you move forward with confidence. £8.99 from www.authenticmedia.co.uk.

Chapter 17 / Engaging with your community

Prepare for action

• **Shaftesbury's *Why Social Action?*,** a series of four Bible studies, will help you to develop strong biblical foundations for any community action. Also our *Prayer – Action – Reflection* Cycle helps give a model of action to use on your journey. See www.shaftesburysociety.org.

• **Faithworks** produce a Church Audit Pack to evaluate your church and its potential to rise to the challenge of effective, sustainable community development. They also have a DVD for small groups which includes questions and Bible

passages to help your church to think about how you can serve your wider community.
See *ichurch: Intelligent Church in the 21st Century* from www.faithworks.info.

• **The Naked Church,** produced by GWEINI (the council for the Christian voluntary sector in Wales) addresses the opportunities and challenges facing Christian welfare initiatives in Wales today providing an invaluable introduction to community development principles for churches everywhere. £4.95 from www.gweini.org.uk.

• **'Expressions: the DVD 1'.** Stories of church for a changing culture. Skater church... cell church... messy church... All over the country Christians are beginning new initiatives to connect with those who are currently outside church. This DVD contains 15 stories of these fresh expressions and describes some of the lessons learned so far. £12.99 from www.chpublishing.co.uk.

• **'Expressions: the DVD 2'.**

Changing church in every place. Fresh expressions are flourishing in all types of places ... where you live, worship and work. All over the country Christians are beginning new initiatives to connect with those who are currently outside church. Presented by Diane Louise Jordan, this DVD focuses on four specific areas where fresh expressions of church are breaking new ground. Each film looks at fresh expressions with a distinct focus: sacramental, youth, rural, and work and leisure. £14.99 from www.chpublishing.co.uk.

• **The Relevant Church.** New communities of faith are popping up around the world and are challenging the traditional church model. *The Relevant Church* shares individual ideas and stories of churches that are engaging a new generation with passionate worship and a life-changing message, all while they impact their communities and change their world. £9.99 from www.equippingthechurch.co.uk.

• **Church, Community and Change** is a Tearfund resource and training programme that enables churches to respond to the needs of their communities in a way that shows God's love and brings about real, lasting and positive change. For a free introductory booklet with more detail please email enquiry@tearfund.org or call 0845 355 8355. When you sign up for the programme you are assigned a facilitator to help you run the course at your church.

• **Compassionate Community Work,**

Dave Andrews. This book offers an introductory course on Christlike community work that can be used in both formal and informal settings. £15 from www.micahnetwork.org.

Tools to help you engage and research your community

• **Shaftesbury's *Information Triangle*** explains the points in this chapter in more detail. You can download more information on Shaftesbury's *Information Triangle* at www.shaftesburysociety.org.

• **Shaftesbury's *Questionnaire Pack*** will thoroughly equip you to carry out a community survey and Faithworks also have available a *Community Audit Pack* which contains excellent advice to carry out an audit of your community.

Shaftesbury's Community Mission team:
Jill Clark – Community Mission Co-ordinator.
Tel: 0845 330 6033
Email: communityinfo@shaftesbury society.org
Web: www.shaftesburysociety.org/ communitymission
Faithworks:
Tel: 020 7450 9031
Email: info@faithworks.info
Web: www.faithworks.info

Training

Faithworks run training courses that can be delivered as one day or half day workshops in your area to help your church develop its role within the local community. It covers four practical modules on turning your vision into reality, being distinctly Christian, grant applications and

business planning plus working in partnership with others. Find out more at www.faithworks.info or by emailing info@faithworks.info.

Shaftesbury run bi-monthly training courses in both London and Bradford on issues relating to Christian social action and community development. Some are very practical like how to manage volunteers or deal with conflict and some are theological and ask questions like 'How can the Bible be made relevant in an urban context?' Most of the days are free. Find out more at www.shaftesburysociety. org/communitymission or by emailing jclark@shaftesburysociety.org.

Chapter 19 / Preparing your church for HOPE

Leadership and church auditing

Books
Winning Ways – How to create a culture of outreach in your church, Philip Jinadu and David Lawrence. In this unique and challenging book a pastor and an evangelist combine forces to point a new way forward. *Winning Ways* provides a fresh model of 'evangelistic leadership' that is both biblical and tested, drawing on material developed and shaped in real-life church situations over a number of years. This is a book for leaders and congregations alike who have a heart for mission, and who long for an approach to outreach that is organic, empowering and, above all, effective. Published by

Authentic Media. £8.99 from www.authenticmedia.co.uk.
Online audits
The 'Winning Ways Leaders Consultation' is an online church health and outreach audit. Using a combination of presentation and guided discussion questions on the issues of discipleship, community and outreach, the consultation provides leaders with a personalised and graphical picture of church health and strategy, with recommendations for development. Available at www.winningwaysweb.com.

Developing gifts

• **Church Growth Academy.** This is an 18-month to two-year process for developing people with a motivation for outreach. It helps produce grassroots evangelistic leaders, and can be started before HOPE, or during HOPE. It uses DVD teaching, personal development goals, resources for church life and access to an online community for models of good practice, discussion and help. For more information and a special HOPE 08 package, please visit www.winningwaysweb.com.

Church consultants

• **If your church is part of a denomination,** then chances are good that there will be some regional ministries set aside to provide an outside perspective for local churches. They may not use the 'consultant' terminology, but look for evangelism advisers, regional superintendents, area team and the like.

• **Para-church organisations** sometimes provide specific church health and strategy audits for churches. Try contacting those in your local area.

• **Alternatively, consult** the *UK Christian Handbook* for a list of independent, freelance church consultants. (Available from Christian bookshops.)

• **RUN – Reaching Unchurched Network** is a growing network of churches passionate about mission in contemporary culture. Members of RUN have access to leading edge outreach thinking and up to date ideas, high quality resources and links with churches and ministries across the UK and beyond to benefit from a wide range of experience. Find out more and join RUN (annual subscription £44 for churches or individuals) at www.run.org.uk

'Imagine – how we can reach the UK', DVD presented by Mark Greene, £10. A 50-minute film about integrating faith with the whole of life, helping your church have a bigger impact and living well as fruitful missionaries – www.licc.org.uk/bookshop.

Evangelistic training initiatives

• *Blowing your Cover* by Kevin Higham and Mike Sprenger. This six-part training course on lifestyle evangelism covers communicating the gospel, connecting with your culture and living a Spirit-filled life. Many resources are available to help you run the course including a *Leader's Guide* (£30), a media DVD pack (£45), a *Blowing Your Cover Workbook* (£7 for one, £30 for a pack of five) and a church resource pack which contains everything you would need to run the course for 15 people (£140, saving £25 on buying

individually). For more information and a free sampler DVD see www.blowingyourcover.com.

• **CaFE.** Catholic Faith Exploration (CaFE) run a series called *Pass It On* to help church groups consider their role as evangelists and learn how to run outreach programmes. The course consists of five talks (four x 20 minutes and one x 40 minutes) available on video or audio, a course manual which includes small group discussion questions and a *Pass It On* book taking a more comprehensive look at evangelism. For more details and to order see www.faithcafe.org.

• **DNA.** Part of the Pioneer Trust, DNA is full-time programme running yearly from October– August training you in culturally relevant evangelism and church-based discipleship.

You must be at least eighteen years old to take part in DNA but there is no upper age limit.

You can find out more and apply online at www.dna-uk.org.

• *Genetik – The Message Trust.* The Tribe Academy is based at the Message Trust and aims to train and equip eighteen to twenty five-year-old evangelists in creative arts and urban mission. In 2008, the Message Trust are raising their game and attempting to deliver HOPE schools missions linked into local churches right across Greater Manchester and huge community action weekends in all ten boroughs. In order to be right at the heart of the action, The Message is offering a special year out. Six months training and equipping as part of the Genetik programme followed by six months hands-on as part of a HOPE 08 team in the schools and estates across the region running from September 2007 to August 2008, or January 2008 to December 2008. For more information contact Genetik@message.org.uk – www.message.org.uk.

• J John and the Philo Trust.

Breaking News is a six-week evangelistic training book that can be used by individuals, small groups and whole churches. The sessions provide you with a readymade training programme to engage you and your church in evangelism. Individual copies are £4.99 but prices are reduced for bulk orders. Please see www.philotrust.com or call 01923 287777.

• Lost for Words. *Lost for Words* is

a resource to help people of every age share their faith naturally. It includes three separate courses (children, youth and adults) with leader's notes, a CD Rom with PowerPoint presentations, handouts, activities and publicity material. Available from CPAS for £39.95, tel: 01926 458458.

• Urban Saints in conjunction with Church Pastoral Aid Society and London School of Theology.

Christian Life and Children is a series of six sessions on video to teach about evangelism with children. Each session has three sections to be followed by discussion, Bible study and prayer and the course covers topics including how children grow spiritually, how to build healthier families inside and outside the church, and developing a strategy for effective children's work. Package including video, notes and CD Rom

costs £20. See www.urbansaints.org for more details.

• YFC – The Art of Connecting.

This Youth for Christ course looks at evangelism from the point of view of three stories: yours, your friends and God's. Over the seven weeks, it helps you to see the value of your own testimony and experiences, to listen better to others and to work out how to tell God's story.
Leader's pack (£29 plus £3 p&p) includes leader's guide with activities, discussion starters and interactive teaching, a video and CD to motivate young people to share their story,
The Art of Connecting paperback book, and a set of cards to be given out upon completion of the course. See www.theartofconnecting.org or www.yfc.co.uk for more detail.

• YWAM. Youth With A Mission

run a School of Evangelism course that includes looking at character, understanding the good news, and how to effectively communicate it. The course consists of 13 weeks' study followed by a 12-month outreach programme. See www.ywam-england.com for more details.

• Evangelism Explosion run a

number of courses for both church leaders and congregation members. See www.ee-gb.org.uk for more details.

Books for evangelism

• Just walk across the room,

Bill Hybels. Simple steps pointing people to faith. Zondervan £6.99. From Christian bookshops.

• Sharing Jesus in a new millennium,

Rob Frost. Distilling the wisdom gained from 15 years of experience, Rob Frost examines the place of evangelism in contemporary society and sets out the biblical base for mission. Included are hot tips on the kinds of outreach that really work. £5, available from www.sharejesusinternational.com.

• Sharing the Feast, Anna

Robbins. 'Recipes for evangelism and discipleship for today's church'. Available at £7.99 from store. www.springharvest.org.

• Becoming a Contagious Christian , Bill Hybels and Mark

Mittelberg and *Building a Contagious Church*, Mark Mittelberg – A range of Zondervan books and DVDs are available on these titles.

• You're an angel: Being yourself and sharing your faith, Peter Neilson. This book

aims to encourage and reassure all Christians that they can share their faith without fear. Published by Covenanters - £11.95 from www.amazon.co.uk.

• Beyond the Fringe – Reaching people outside the church, Nick

Pollard. Published by Inter-Varsity Press. £5.99.

• Telling the Story, Luis Palau

and Timothy L. Robnett. If you've ever wondered 'Have I been called to be an evangelist?' and 'Where do I begin?' this book is for you. A valuable resource for anyone contemplating the call to evangelism, this book includes an extensive appendix with spiritual gifts inventories, directories of

evangelistic networks, and checklists for the growing ministry. £10.49 from www.equippingthechurch.co.uk.

• **Dare 2 Share – A Field Guide to Sharing Your Faith,** Greig Stier. This practical handbook focuses on conversation starters, compliments, common ground and the skill of listening, plus helps readers identify their natural style of evangelism and shows you how to defend your faith without offending others. £10.99 from www.equippingthechurch.co.uk.

• **Permission Evangelism,** Michael Simpson. Evangelism without the fear! This book uses proven business and marketing techniques to encourage evangelism. £7.99 from www.equippingthechurch.co.uk.

• **50 Ways to Share Your Faith,** Ian Knox. Christians know that people need Jesus but often panic at the thought of sharing their faith. Ian Knox has been an evangelist for many years and here shares his mistakes with us as well as his successes in the hope that we will be encouraged in our evangelistic efforts and ultimately know the joy of leading someone to Christ. £8.99 from www.equippingthechurch.co.uk.

• **The Evangelist's Notebook,** John Peters. John looks at what it takes to be an evangelist and shares his own experiences, urging us to concentrate on the essential truths in our evangelism and to be open to the Spirit's leading in our conversations with unbelievers. Published by Kingsway. £8.99 from www.equippingthechurch.co.uk.

• **Ambiguous Evangelism,** Bob Mayo with Sylvie Collins and Sara Savage. In this practical and encouraging book, Bob Mayo helps us to examine evangelism in a culture where people know very little about the Christian faith. £9.99 from www.spck.org.uk.

• **Reaching Single Adults: An Essential Guide for Ministry,** Dennis Franck. A comprehensive handbook to help your church reach the 44 per cent of adults who are unmarried. £9.99 from www.eden.co.uk.

• **40 Days of Community,** Rick Warren. The latest in The Purpose Driven Life series, this book helps churches deepen authentic community within their church family and reach out to the local community outside the church. Find out more at www.purposedriven.co.uk.

FURTHER RESOURCES FOR EVANGELISM

• **You can download** a free ten-page PDF file on evangelism from the Christians in Sport website www.christiansinsport.org.uk.

• **The Godman** is a 3D animation film that presents the gospel story of Jesus as the Saviour in a way that is accessible to children. You can purchase '*The Godman* Mission Pack' for £49.99 which includes the DVD, promotional materials for your church and 200 copies of the *Children's Animated Edition of the Book of Hope* to complement the film. Find out more at www.bookofhope.co.uk and order at www.UCB2GO.co.uk.

• **'In motion'** is an 80-minute DVD designed for use within church services, small groups and outreach events which explores the themes of forgiveness, success, relationships and spirituality to provoke a response to the Christian message. £20 (incl. p&p) from www.run.org.uk.

• **Game of Life** – An evangelistic resource from J John expressing the Christian message through sport. Single copy £1.99, bulk buy from 45p from www.philotrust.com.

• **UCB's** *Looking for God?* initiative takes people through a unique, internet-based presentation of the gospel, gives them an opportunity to respond and provides practical, personal support to anyone making a decision to accept Christ. See www.lookingforGod.com.

• **THE4POINTS** is a simple but effective way of communicating the gospel with people regardless of age or background. Resources with the 4points symbols include T-shirts, wristbands, balloons, canvas banners, car stickers and badges. Find out more and purchase items at www.4points.co.uk.

Miscellaneous

• **Inspire** is the UK's fastest growing 'good news' magazine, telling uplifting stories of God at work in individuals, churches and communities every month. It's free to churches and available to order in bundles of ten from www.inspiremagazine.org.uk.

• **New Life** is a monthly newspaper with issues packed with real-life testimonies and celebrity interviews, helping you reach your community with the gospel. They can even supply copies featuring your own local news. Bulk copies from as little as 17p each, and individual subscriptions from only £10.00 for one year. To order copies or for further information call 0115 921 7280, email info@newlifepublishing.co.uk or visit www.newlifenewspaper.co.uk.

• **Urban Saints** run one-day training conferences on a number of different topics. See www.urbansaints.org for the latest news.

• **Many organisations** will make speakers, evangelists, worship leaders and drama/dance/theatre/music teams available for HOPE 08 events. See www.hope08.com for more details.

• Books are available direct from the publisher's website as stated or from Christian bookshops such as:

- Christian Bits – www.christianbits.co.uk
- Christian Book Exchange – www.cbebooks.org
- Eden – www.eden.co.uk
- Grove Books – www.grovebooks.co.uk
- Wesley Owen – www.wesleyowen.com
- St Andrew's – www.standrewsbookshop.co.uk
- The Good Bookstall – www.thegoodbookstall.org.uk
- You can find your nearest Christian bookshop at www.christianbookshops.org.uk

NOTE: HOPE 08 is not responsible for the content of third party websites and resources. Prices were correct at time of going to print.

CHAPTER 21

ACKNOWLEDGEMENTS

Board of Reference

Matt Baggott
Chief Constable Leicestershire & Association of Chief Police Officers

Fran Beckett
CEO of Church Urban Fund

Rev David Coffey
President of the Baptist World Alliance

Rev Joel Edwards
General Director of Evangelical Alliance

Rev Nicky Gumbel
Holy Trinity Brompton & Alpha International

Commissioner Elizabeth Matear
Moderator of Free Church Council

His Eminence Cardinal Cormac Murphy O'Connor
Archbishop of Westminster

Caroline Spelman MP
Shadow Communities & Local Government

Lord John Stevens
Former Commissioner of Metropolitan Police Service

Rt Hon Stephen Timms MP
Chief Secretary to HM Treasury

Steve Webb MP
Health Spokesman

'Advocacy & Advisory Board'

Rev. Dr. Martyn Atkins
Cliff College

Mr. Don Axcell
CPA

Mgr. Keith Barltrop
Catholic Agency to Support Evangelisation

Mr. Stuart Bell
Ground Level

Mr. Jonathan Bellamy
Cross Rhythms

Mrs. Mary Bishop
Groom Shaftesbury

Rev. Lyndon Bowring
CARE

Mr. James Catford
Bible Society

Rev. Steve Chalke MBE
Oasis Trust

Mr. Keith Civval
Scripture Union

Mr. Gerald Coates
Pioneer Trust

Rev. Dr. David Cornick
United Reform Church

Rev. John Dunnett
CPAS

Rev. Jonathan Edwards
Baptist Union

Mr. Roger Ellis
Revelation

Mr. Matthew Frost
Tearfund

Rev. Dr. Rob Frost
Share Jesus International

Rev. John Glass
Elim

Mr. & Mrs. Ray & Nancy Goudie
NGM

Mrs. Debra Green
Redeeming Our Communities

Mr. Ian Hamilton
Compassion UK

Mr. David Heron
Premier Media Group

Mr. Paul Hopkins
Youth With A Mission

Miss. Katei Kirby
Afro-Carribean Evangelical Alliance

Commissioner John Matear
Salvation Army

Mr. Simon Matthews
Plumbline International

Mr. Tim Morfin
The Lighthouse Group

Rev. Nims Obunge
The Peace Alliance

Mr. John Paculabo
Kingsway Communications

Mr. Rob Parsons
Care for the Family

Mr. Patrick Regan
XLP

Rev. Bill Slack
BU of Scotland

Mr. Matt Summerfield
Urban Saints

Mr. Steve Thomas
Salt & Light

Rev. Paul Weaver
AOG

Associate Groups*

24-7 Prayer
ACEA (African and Caribbean Evangelical Alliance)
ALOVE UK
Alpha
Assemblies Of God
Audacious
Baptist Union
Bible Society
Big Idea
Book of Hope
BT Christian Network
Care
Care For The Family
Case
Cell UK
Christian Enquiry Agency
Christian Workplace Forum
Church Action on Poverty
Church Army
Church of England
Church of Scotland
Compassion
CORD
Coventry Cathedral
Cross Rhythms
Elim Church
Evangelical Alliance
Evangelical Alliance - Northern Ireland
Evangelical Alliance - Scotland
Evangelical Alliance – Wales
Every Home for Christ UK
Extreme Hope
Faithworks
Fresh Expressions
Fusion
GEAR (Grp for Evangelism And Renewal in URC)
God TV
Ground Level
Gweini
Ichthus
Ignite
Innervation

Jubilee Trust
Kingdom Faith
Kingsway Communication
Lambeth Palace
Luis Palau Association
Mainstream
Makeway Music
Micah Challenge
Methodist Church
NE1
New Generation Ministries
New Wine
N:VISION
NXT Ministries
Oasis
Operation Mobilisation (UK)
Pioneer
Premier Radio
Reality Leicester
Redeeming Our Communities
ReJesus
ReSource
Rhema Theatre Company
RUN
Salt + Light
Saltmine
Salvation Army
Samaritans Purse
Scripture Union
Send The Light - Wesley Owen
Serious 4 God
Shaftesbury Society
Share Jesus
Soul Survivor
SOULINTHECITY LONDON
South West Youth Ministries
Spring Harvest
Student Christian Movement
Tearfund
The Message
The Net
Through Faith Missions
Together for the Harvest
Together in Mission
United Christian Broadcasters

United Reformed Church
Urban Saints
Vineyard
Vision 2025
World Prayer Centre
YES
Youth For Christ
Youth With A Mission

*List correct at time of going to print, please see www.hope08.com for the most up-to-date list of Associate Groups as new members are joining all the time.

Board/Leadership Team

Laurence Singlehurst
CELL UK

Paul Bayes
Church of England

Ian Chisnall
HOPE 08

Fritha Wheeler
HOPE 08

Matt Bird
Make It Happen

Steve Clifford
Pioneer Network/Soul Survivor

Mike Pilavachi
Soul Survivor

Dave Poultney
Soul Survivor

Eustace Constance
Street Pastors

Andy Hawthorne
The Message

Roy Crowne
YFC

Sarah Davis
YFC

Clive Dudbridge
YFC

Martin Kavanagh
World Harvest Bible Church

Jane Holloway
World Prayer Centre

Contributors

Many thanks to

All the writers in this publication:

David Arscott, Paul Bayes, Matt Bird, Dee Buchanan, Gavin Calver, Ian Chisnall, Steve Clifford, Rob Cotton, Roy Crowne, Dan Etheridge, Andy Hawthorne, Ian Henderson, Jane Holloway, Liza Hoeksma, Phil Hulks, Philip Jinadu, Jon Kuhrt, Mike Pilavachi, Julian Richards, Richard Shaw, Laurence Singlehurst and Marty Woods.

The following for contributions, advice and support:

Jonathan Bellamy, Tania Bright, Jill Clark, Phil Collins, Sarah Davis, Clive Dudbridge, Andy Flannagan, Sue Green, Becs Gumbel, Kim Hardiker, Lynn Howson, Lee Jackson, Martin Kavanagh, Alison Maffey, Dave Newton, Jenny Seal, Helen Share, Kate Smith, David Spriggs, Rebecca Stewart and Cathy Webber.

To the photographers who provided us with images:

Howard Barlow, Jon Bullock, Martin Butcher, Ann Clifford, Cornerstone, Andy Espin, Becks Heyhoe, HTB/Alpha, Andrew Phillips, Mike Thorpe.

The Board and Leadership team of HOPE 08 wish to express their gratitude to the Management Team at Authentic Media and Wesley Owen. It has been thanks to their sacrificial support that this publication has been possible. Particular thanks to Keith Danby, Malcolm Down and Dave Withers.

A huge thanks to everyone who is on board with HOPE 08, including every one of you who has bought this publication. This initiative belongs to all the churches, organisations and individuals across the UK who will make HOPE 08 happen.

Design

Many thanks to ABA design for the HOPE 08 logo and to Mike Thorpe/ The Design Chapel for designing this publication.

Contact us

HOPE 08 Office
Unit 4, Fairway Business Park
Westergate Road
Brighton
BN2 4JZ
Telephone: 01273 571939
Fax: 01273 626345
Email: info@hope08.com
Website: www.hope08.com

Hope 08 Ltd is a Charity (No. 1116005) and a Company Limited by Guarantee (No. 5801431)

First published 2007 by Authentic Media

9 Holdom Avenue, Bletchley, Milton Keynes, Bucks, MK1 1QR, UK
1820 Jet Stream Drive, Colorado Springs, CO 80921, USA
OM Authentic Media, Medchal Road, Jeedimetla Village, Secunderabad 500 055, A.P., India
www.authenticmedia.co.uk
Authentic Media is a division of IBS-STL U.K., a company limited by guarantee (registered charity no. 270162)

British Library Cataloguing in Publication Data
A catalogue record for this book is available from the British Library
ISBN-13: 978-1-86024-613-5